DROP SHIP
SECRETS

DROP SHIP
SECRETS

The Ultimate Playbook For Starting a Highly Profitable, Semi-Automated Store From Anywhere In The World

BY: ANTON KRALY

About This Book

Hi, I'm Anton Kraly, serial entrepreneur and founder of Drop Ship Lifestyle. My company was created to give students the knowledge and tools necessary to create freedom through entrepreneurship by leveraging the power of drop shipping.

Our courses, one-on-one coaching, online communities, software, annual retreats, and now this book, are all designed to help those seeking a different path in life.

For some, that means the ability to spend more quality time with their families or children. For others, it means being able to travel the world and work from anywhere with a reliable WiFi connection.

This book will guide you through the business model and the step-by-step method anyone can use to create a successful online business.

The Method

Building and growing dozens of eCommerce stores in multiple niches with thousands of suppliers and products is a challenge. Especially when you don't have a proper system to follow.

These challenges are what originally led me to create the 7-Step Drop Ship Blueprint. My drop shipping method that I teach today started as an internal document for my company to reference when researching new niches, doing market research, building stores, getting approved with suppliers, optimizing for conversions, getting traffic, as well as outsourcing and automating.

This streamlined approach to eCommerce lead to exponential growth, and in 2012, I began sharing my Blueprint with the world.

And now, for the first time ever, I'm sharing my methods for high-ticket drop shipping in physical form with a book that will guide you to eCommerce success.

I put this book together with one goal in mind: to help you start your own highly-profitable, semi-automated drop ship store.

Inside this book, you'll learn the business model and how drop shipping works before hearing a few of my favorite stories from members of the community.

Then I'll go into the finer points of my method of building a drop shipping business that lasts. In the back of this book, you'll find several pages of additional resources such as a Glossary and Niche Selection Checklist.

Table of Contents

ABOUT THIS BOOK 4

INTRODUCTION 9

PART 1: THE MODEL

How Drop Shipping Works. 17
7 Steps to Building a Successful Drop Shipping Store 20
          Common Drop Shipping Mistakes to Avoid 23
          Advantages of Drop Shipping. 29
          Disadvantages of Drop Shipping 32
Frequently Asked Questions 34

PART 2: THE METHOD

Will I Be Successful with Drop Shipping? 40
          Is Drop Shipping Worth it? 42
          What is Your "Why?". 45
          How Much Money Can I Expect to Make? 46
Where Will I Sell My Products?. 51

Where to Build Your Drop Shipping Store. 57

What Products Should I Sell? 60

    Niche Selection Criteria. 62

    Niche Selection Methods. 68

    3X Your Niche List. 73

    Testing Your Niche 75

How to Find Drop Ship Suppliers. 78

    The 3 Tiers of Suppliers You Will Want to Work With . . .82

    Getting Approved by Drop Ship Suppliers 84

    How to Contact Suppliers 87

How Will I Get People to Buy From My Store? 91

    The Right Type of Traffic 92

    Identifying Your Market Segment. 96

    The Customer Avatar: What is it? 99

    Building Your Customer Avatar in 5 Steps. 102

    Lead Value Optimization. 108

RESOURCES

Niche Selection Checklist 114

Competitor Research Table 126

Competitor Analysis 131

Your Customer Avatar 134

Glossary 136

Introduction

Inspired by my successful uncle, at age 14, I had decided that I was going to be an entrepreneur. I grew up in Long Island in a middle-class family and I had a great childhood, but I was always dreaming of bigger things. I didn't want to just survive... I wanted to thrive.

In 2006, right after I graduated college, I developed a plan to become an entrepreneur. That plan was to...

- Open an offline business

- Work 80+ hours a week building an empire

- Sell that empire by the time I was 40

- Then, retire 'young' and travel the world

My first business venture was a cookie delivery route that I bought. I would go around New York City selling baked goods to local coffee shops and grocery stores. At first I was pumped! The cookie biz had so much potential.

However, it wasn't long before I grew tired of the New York City traffic and the tiny margins that came with selling cookies to local grocery stores. I started to realize this business was not right for me.

Yes, this was my first business, but it was not the "lifestyle" I had envisioned for myself. I knew things had to change if I ever wanted to make serious money and become a well-traveled entrepreneur.

Lucky for me, a friend recommended a book that was taking the world by storm, and honestly, still is. It's called *The 4-Hour Workweek* by Tim Ferris. I read it in 2007 when that book only had one chapter on eCommerce, but it opened up my eyes to what was possible in the early days of the internet.

Building off inspiration, I built my first drop shipping store selling cookies. I started selling the cookies from my delivery route online, and the bakery would fulfill the orders for me. It was very successful, but I saw more potential to make money with this business model.

So, I built another drop shipping store, but I went through Alibaba to sell more expensive products. Just two years later, I sold my first eCommerce store.

In my first year with these 'high-ticket' drop shipping stores, I did over $300,000 in sales. My second year, over $680,000! Then, in my third year I hit the million dollar mark, and did $1.2 million in sales from my drop shipping store. By my fourth year, I reached $1.8 million dollars in sales.

I eventually started selling off my stores. (One of my first drop shipping stores sold for $650,000!) Finally, I was the entrepreneur that I dreamed of when I was a teenager.

My Quest for Drop Shipping Knowledge

I was making these sales back when I didn't know much about anything. Even though I wasn't an expert, I was willing to learn about eCommerce and willing to take risks. As I learned more and more, I started to think, "Maybe there are other people out there that I could connect with. There must be other drop shipping business owners that I can learn from."

So I went to Google and searched for eCommerce and drop shipping communities. Unfortunately, what I found were a bunch of people who were only pretending like they knew it all.

I could tell from my real world experience of generating seven figure businesses, that these people didn't know what they were talking about. They were just hoping to sell their or latest eBook or hoping for 'free' private coaching.

I started thinking that I obviously knew more than these people, but none of their followers knew enough to call them out and say, "Hey, this doesn't work!" And back in 2012, that's what I started doing. I started posting on those forums where I found outdated, nonsense information, saying, "This is wrong and here's how to fix your drop shipping business."

I started sharing my method for finding products to drop ship–even going as far as sharing a better approach for how to get suppliers and paid traffic. I was sharing everything I had learned over the years, mostly through trial and error.

How I Became a Drop Shipping Authority

People started responding. They would message me, try to get on Skype with me, or they would email and say, "Listen, Anton, you obviously know what you're talking about. Can I pay you for coaching?"

At first, I said, no. That's not what I wanted to do. I didn't want to be someone's coach where I was on the phone with them every week. But then I had the idea to take all of what I know about building an eCommerce business, and put it into a series of helpful videos.

I also wanted an online community where everyone would be learning, building their stores, and connecting on the same level.

That's when I first thought to turn this into a private community of people committed to learning eCommerce from me and my trainings. This community could engage in high level conversation about drop shipping. It would be a place where everyone could grow, practice, and get better. This became the first version of Drop Ship Lifestyle.

Drop Ship Lifestyle 1.0

It's been several years since I started Drop Ship Lifestyle, and over the years, this community has grown to more than 8,000 people from at least 30 different countries. It's just insane to me that this is what Drop Ship Lifestyle has become! I couldn't be happier.

In 2017, what I always knew was made official: Drop Ship Lifestyle was voted as the "Best eCommerce Course" as part of Shopify's annual Commerce Awards. For this category, the judges were looking for the best in user-friendly, educational, and inspirational eCommerce courses.

The reason Drop Ship Lifestyle has grown so much over the past five years is because our students are the best drop shippers in the world, and our community is the best in the world.

There are tons of online business courses and programs out there, but I'm telling you... what we have here at Drop Ship Lifestyle is special.

If you go on our YouTube channel, blog, or our Facebook page, you'll see hundreds of success stories from people all around the world. They changed their lives by following my Drop Ship Blueprint and because they were supported by the amazing DSL community.

My team and I measure our success by the success of our members. We track this via our social media pages, our email inboxes, feedback from our live events, and letters that are sent to our offices.

Whether you're looking to supplement your income, replace your income, or increase your total earnings, my goal with Drop Ship Lifestyle is to provide you with the training, support, and community that you need to get there.

PART 1
THE MODEL

How Drop Shipping Works

What do you think drop shipping is?

_____

_____

Drop shipping is a retail method where you don't keep products in stock. Instead, you partner with a supplier that stocks its own inventory. You transfer customer orders and shipment details to them, and the suppliers ship the order directly to the customer.

That's it. **You don't handle shipping or inventory!** You as a drop shipper simply get orders from customers and pass those orders on to suppliers.

Now, your goal as a drop shipping retailer is to get approved with good suppliers that make quality products.

Once you are approved, these suppliers let you sell their products on your website. You make the sale, and then the supplier receives a notification from you to ship the item to the anticipating customer.

THE DROP SHIPPING BUSINESS MODEL

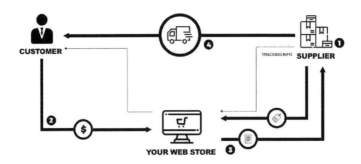

Step 1: You list the supplier's product on your store for customers to buy.

Step 2: The customer purchases something from your eCommerce store.

Step 3: You order that same exact item that the customer paid for from your supplier.

Step 4: Your drop shipping supplier ships this item directly to your customer. So your customer receives the item that they've ordered from you.

The previous image shows the drop shipping process, but let me break it down a bit further for you. It starts with building your own eCommerce store and listing products on your website. You create this store on Shopify and customize it to fit your audience.

But whose products are you selling? Remember, you're selling different suppliers' and brands' products.

You may be thinking, "Why don't these companies sell their products directly?" There are companies that only focus on innovating products that rely on retailers to sell them.

That's where you come in as a drop ship retailer, you'll be selling for these brands who don't sell to the public. They look for people to sell their products, to make them money, and grow their business for them.

You are one of these retailers. You'll want to focus on getting approved to sell for different companies. After you're approved, you'll put their products on your Shopify store. Then you will advertise to bring people to your store. Once somebody buys a product listed on your store, you contact your suppliers.

The supplier then ships the items directly to the customer. You aren't buying any inventory. All you're doing is making an agreement with the drop ship supplier to sell their products on your website.

You get their price lists and put their products for sale on your site. You only order the product after the customer has paid you. Then you'll contact that supplier, and say "Ship item XYZ to customer ABC." Then they ship it and charge you.

The difference between your retail price and your expenses is called the **net profit**. From my experience, when you drop ship the right way, you're looking at about 25 to 30 percent average net profit. That means if you sell a $1,000 item, you can make about $300. Sometimes it's higher, sometimes it's lower, but that's a good goal to shoot for. It's a realistic expectation.

Now that you have a good overview of what drop shipping is, you're ready to see the seven steps to being successful in eCommerce. The next part of this book covers the seven steps you can follow to create a successful drop shipping store.

7 Steps to Building a Successful Drop Shipping Store

There are lots of ways to sell with eCommerce and drop shipping– just like anything else. But I want to give you a brief overview of the system I use when creating new drop ship stores in Shopify. I've been doing this for over a decade now, and these steps continue to work.

Think of these seven steps as a checklist for every time you build a new drop shipping store. If you follow the steps and do the work, you'll find success.

7 STEPS TO BUILDING A **SUCCESSFUL** DROP SHIPPING **STORE**

1 CHOOSE A NICHE

2 RESEARCH FUTURE COMPETITORS

3 CREATE YOUR STORE

4 GET APPROVED BY SUPPLIERS

5 OPTIMIZE YOUR SITE FOR CONVERSIONS

6 TURN ON PAID TRAFFIC

7 OUTSOURCE AND AUTOMATE YOUR TASKS

Step #1 is all about finding the right niche (the specific set of products you'll be selling). The key to finding a good niche is to be specific. Your goal shouldn't be to sell a bunch of different products. We have no interest in trying to be Amazon. Stick to a specific niche, and you'll find the later steps much easier. You'll also end up making more money with your store.

Step #2 is researching your future competitors. And It's easier than you think! You're going to go online and find websites that are already selling in a prospective niche. Then you need to find out a couple things about those sites– like if they have a warehouse, showroom, or retail stores. The goal is to find companies that sell online for multiple brands but have no physical presence. This shows you that they're drop ship suppliers. It means you can compete with them!

Step #3 is all about setting up your store (yes before you've even found your suppliers)! You have to be able to show the suppliers where you will be selling their products. That way, they actually approve you, and we can move on to the next step. This builds trust with your potential suppliers, so they'll want to work with you.

Step #4 is finding suppliers for your niche and getting approved to sell for them. You do this by reaching out by phone and email. This is where you'll show them the store you built in Step #3. It may take a little bit of time and perseverance to finally get your suppliers, but keep at it. The work will pay off.

Step #5 is all about optimizing for conversions. Basically, it's doing certain things to get more people buying AND make more from each person.

Step #6 is all about bringing people to your store. There are definitely techniques for bringing more traffic to your website but the real trick is getting good, quality traffic. This way, you're getting the most out of the money you're spending.

There are many sources of traffic for drop shipping, but if you don't want to waste a bunch of money, you should focus on a few of the best.

The channels that bring in the highest quality traffic are Google PLAs, influencer marketing, and very basic SEO. I don't recommend spending money on SEO. You can do most of it yourself and be profitable.

Step #7 to building a successful drop shipping store is to start outsourcing and automating tasks. Only do this step after:

- You found your niche

- You built your store

- You got approved with suppliers

- You optimize it for conversions

- You have traffic coming in

- *And you're making money*

Most of this last step is achieved by using apps and plugins that will automate day-to-day tasks for you. That way, you don't have to work as much and still make money.

The second part of this step is outsourcing. Basically, you'll want to hire remote workers (virtual assistants) to take over some of the basic repetitive tasks. The end goal is to set up a business that's semi-automated so you can work as little or as much as you want.

These are the seven steps that I use to make my stores profitable. It's what I teach in my course, and it's what has worked for a decade! Now that I briefly covered what you should do to be profitable, I want to talk about what you should avoid.

Common Drop Shipping Mistakes to Avoid

There's a lot of bad information online about drop shipping. This leads to people making costly mistakes that can kill their drop shipping business. If you want to have a successful drop shipping business, avoid these five mistakes. These five can completely derail your business before you even start.

Mistake #1: Paying for Access to a Supplier

If you search for "drop ship suppliers" on Google, you're going to find that most of the companies that pop up are middlemen.

Middlemen Suppliers: Companies that make most of their money from fees that they charge you. These are NOT actual suppliers.

Two types of fees that middlemen charge:

1. Application fee for you to work with them.

2. Drop ship fees for orders you place with them.

These suppliers aren't looking for a long-term business relationship. They won't provide a valuable service to you OR your customers. Any company that charges you to sell their products is a middleman. They are making money off these monthly fees and account activations. What's worse is that these products aren't going to sell well and there are going to be a ton of competitors. Never pay for access to a supplier.

A **good supplier** won't charge you for access. If a stand-up supplier approves you as a retailer, they are doing so because they see a value in your service as a retailer. You and your supplier are business partners, of sorts. Both you and your supplier work together for the greater good. You make money, they make money, and everyone is happy.

Good suppliers won't charge you for access to them...that's ridiculous. Stay away from anyone trying to charge you access. Middlemen "drop ship suppliers" are bad news for your drop shipping business.

Mistake #2: Working with Low Quality Suppliers

Usually, when you see the term "drop shipping" online, it's low-ticket products from China. Drop shipping acquired a bad reputation because of drop shipping companies that sell cheap products through irresponsible suppliers.

When good suppliers hear the term "drop shipping," they run. They want nothing to do with the average drop shipper.

Good suppliers want to work with *internet retailers*. Many good internet retailers drop ship, but they don't SAY that they are drop shipping. They simply sell products, and the supplier ships them.

My company is called Drop Ship Lifestyle because I want to pull in the folks searching "drop shipping" on Google. I want to shine a light on the current trends in the drop shipping industry. I hope to show folks that high-ticket drop shipping with good suppliers is an honest and profitable way to do business.

You want to work with suppliers who are building an **actual brand**, and they want to work with you, an internet retailer– not a scammy drop shipper who wants to treat customers horribly and violate the supplier contract.

Mistake #3: Working With Suppliers Who Don't Enforce MAP Policies

The next common mistake to avoid is working with suppliers who don't enforce MAP. MAP is a common term in the industry that stands for minimum advertised price. You want to sell for suppliers who have pricing controls.

It's super important that you ONLY work with suppliers who enforce MAP policies (at least when you're just starting out).

Minimum Advertised Price (MAP) Policies: The minimum amount that a product can be sold for - enforced by the supplier.

Why are MAP Policies Beneficial for Your Drop Ship Store?

You won't get yourself into pricing wars. For example, let's say their brand sells a lady's leather bag and their minimum advertised price is $1000 and your wholesale cost is $600. That means you make $400 per sale. But maybe you're okay with making $200 per sale, so you want to sell for $800.

These suppliers won't let you do that and will ban you. The reason they have these pricing controls is to help their brands hold credibility and value. They aren't going to let retailers constantly undercut each other until no one is making money. And more importantly, until the perceived value of their brand goes down.

That's why you only want to work with suppliers that enforce a minimum advertised price. Thankfully there are a bunch of ways to check if they do. You could just ask your suppliers but there are more automated ways. MAP policies ensure fairness and success. MAP policies protect the supplier's brand and YOUR profit margins.

Mistake #4: Competing with Offline Retailers

Don't try to compete with offline retailers. When you're looking for future competitors, avoid companies that have physical stores or warehouses. They are most likely going to get better pricing from suppliers and be able to sell for less.

Also, if someone has the option of buying something online or going down the block and picking it up the same day, they will most likely choose the latter. One great way to find niches and suppliers is to find unique areas within niches where the products aren't readily available locally.

One quick example is chandeliers. Let's say someone wants to buy a chandelier for their new house. Sure, they can go to Home Depot or Lowe's. They probably can find some chandeliers at local stores, but maybe they can't find the exact one they want.

This is an item that has literally thousands of variations and Home Depot carries about 50 different types. It has hundreds of brands, and not all of them are going to be sold in a local store. This means a customer probably has to buy online.

You'll focus on the brands that are online only. That's because you'll be able to get approved with these brands and actually be able to compete in this space. Just know that you should avoid directly competing with offline retailers.

Mistake #5: Buying a 'Turnkey' Drop Shipping Store

Buying turnkey drop shipping stores is a mistake people make far too often. If you go online to any of these low-end auction websites, you'll find these stores.

They'll claim, "drop ship store, huge opportunity, 5,000 products ready to go." But the truth is... these don't work. They are all just clones of each other.

These sites are just a way for the sellers to make a quick buck. I can't even see myself, someone that has been in drop shipping for over a decade, buying one of those and making it profitable. These are a waste of time and money.

Good eCommerce stores and drop shipping stores exist and are for sale. I have sold them, but they go into the mid-high six figure range, and I don't think anyone reading this is looking to spend half a million dollars on a website right from the start.

Mistake #6: Getting Stuck on Niche Selection

Picking a niche is arguably the most important step in building your drop shipping store. In my course, I ask people to come up with and do research on 50 niches.

This is baffling for many of them. "50 NICHES?! THAT'S INSANE!" Well... it's really not.

Think about your hobbies. Think about your friend's hobbies. Think about your family members' hobbies. What would you and these people buy to support those hobbies?

Mistake #7: Drop Shipping Low-Ticket Products

I want to make one thing clear: selling a $10 iPhone case is just as easy as selling a $1000 paddle board. When I say this, it blows people's minds. However, it's all too true.

As a drop shipper, all you need to do to list products is get approved by a supplier and upload those products to your site. After this, you make sales.

The iPhone case market is oversaturated. It's not easy to make a sale. The paddle board market is not oversaturated. It's niche specific, and only a very specific audience looks to buy paddle boards online. To make $5,000 in sales, you'll need to sell five paddle boards OR sell 500 iPhone cases.

These are both easy things to list on your drop shipping site... So what product do you think will make you more money? With paddle boards, you need less traffic, less conversions, and less ads to make much, much more money.

Mistake #8: Not Creating a Demo Store to Show Suppliers

Would you trust a random person calling you on the phone asking to sell and represent your brand? No. You wouldn't. If you would, you're crazy.

That's why you NEED a demo store if you want to get approved by legit suppliers. This isn't hard. It's not complicated. It's just a demo store, and I promise it will make all the difference.

In my 10+ years of eCommerce experience, this mistake is one that I find to be the most brutal. Having a demo store boosts your chances for success.

Advantages of Drop Shipping

Before I go deeper into how to drop ship, I want to make sure to cover all the benefits and disadvantages of drop shipping. That way, you have clear expectations of the good and bad parts that come with running a drop shipping business.

Location Independence

The first advantage, and probably the one that's most important to me with drop shipping, is being location independent. In the last few years I've lived in and ran drop shipping stores from Vietnam, South America, and Thailand. With a drop shipping business, you really can live and work from wherever you want.

Drop shipping is a viable path to quitting that nine to five job that you despise. If you love your nine to five, drop shipping can even be a way to bolster your bank account! Living the drop ship lifestyle gives you freedom.

No Inventory Costs

Another benefit is that there are no inventory costs. So when you're starting out with drop shipping, you aren't laying out any of your money for inventory.

When you're a traditional retailer, inventory is your biggest expense. You need to physically have the products to sell, but with drop shipping, you don't. All you need is approvals from suppliers to have products. You only pay for items after you sell them, so there are no warehouse costs.

Now in the previous section, I wrote about how I started in eCommerce by importing. So when I first started, I actually had these inventory and warehouse costs. I was spending tons of money every month to store my products.

But if you use the drop shipping business model, you're not paying for these expenses– someone else is. All of your suppliers have their own warehouses, and they're paying to store these items. So it's another cost that isn't on your shoulders– something you don't have to worry about when starting out.

No Handling Returns

Another benefit to drop shipping is not having to handle returns. To be clear, if your customer wants to return an item, you'll still have to forward the return slip from your supplier to your customer.

But these items are not coming to you. If you own a drop shipping business, you won't have returned products showing up at your house.

They're going to be shipped back to your supplier, and then based on the policy of that supplier, you'll get a refund or they'll ship the customer a replacement item.

Gather Data While Getting Paid

This next advantage of drop shipping is gathering data while you're getting paid. Let's say that you want to build a brand in the chandelier niche; you want to sell your own lighting fixtures or chandeliers. Also, let's assume that you want to be an importer and build your own product line. We'll also say that you even have the money to invest in it right now.

Well, before you throw money at an import business, have products manufactured, and start trying to sell them… I'd still recommend that you start a drop shipping business in that niche first.

As you're drop shipping, you'll be learning what sells. You'll be able to find out what your customer wants, and you'll be building resources that you can use for your own product line… all while making money. Basically, you're testing out the market while making a profit.

You'll learn what types of products sell best, what price point you make the most with, and what customers you like to deal with. Then, after you're successful in that niche, you can use all that data to launch your own brand with an importing business.

Easily Scalable

Another huge benefit of a drop shipping business is how easy it is to scale. For instance, if you are making $100,000 a year in sales from just one drop shipping store, it's very easy to build more stores with similar results. And the best part is that you can do this over and over again.

I always recommend starting with one drop shipping store so that you really learn the process, go through it, and master it. But after you do it one time, it's very easy to do it over and over again.

A Drop Shipping Business is a Sellable Asset

Now, when I first started this business, I didn't realize it, but drop shipping stores are very valuable to a lot of people. There are a lot of buyers out there that are looking for profitable eCommerce stores, especially drop shipping stores.

Because in all honesty, these buyers could just plug themselves into your business and be making money the next day– all without having to take over your inventory or take over a warehouse. There's a reason people want to buy these kind of businesses.

Here's an example of what a drop shipping business will sell for:

So let's say at the low end, you build a drop shipping business that's making you $1,000 a month in profit. That's an amount that I think everyone could wrap their heads around, it's very reasonable and attainable.

That store could be worth as high as $20,000. So that is what I mean here when I say drop shipping is one of the best ways to make money online, it's in large part because you're building a real asset.

One great resource for selling your drop shipping business is Empire Flippers. It's a marketplace to buy and sell drop shipping stores in all price ranges, from a couple thousand... to millions.

Disadvantages of Drop Shipping

This model is fantastic, but it's not perfect. That's why, before you dive in, I want you to be honest with you about *all* parts of drop shipping.

Let's talk about some of the disadvantages of owning a drop shipping business when compared to owning your own brand.

Smaller Profit Margins

First off, drop shipping gives you smaller margins. Because you're selling someone else's products, profits are going to be less than if you created your own.

If you go to China and have your products manufactured, you can negotiate better deals for the product price. That's because you're doing a lot more work and taking on a lot more of the responsibility. As a result, your profit margins will be higher.

So with drop shipping, there are usually smaller profit margins than with selling your own brands. Later in this book, I will cover the exact margins. On average, I aim for 25% profit margins with my drop shipping stores.

No Inventory Control

Another thing that's not so great about drop shipping, and in my opinion is probably the biggest downside, is that you have no control over inventory.

Let's say you have one supplier whose product sells well on your website, you're making great money with them. Well, what happens if that supplier runs out of stock? What if your drop shipping supplier sells out of those items?

Your customers are still going to want to order from you, but you won't be able to fulfill these orders. You're going to lose potential money in that situation. All because you have no control over the inventory, or because maybe your suppliers aren't so great about managing inventory and keeping every item in stock.

This is something that great suppliers know how to deal with. Regardless, it's probably something you'll run into at least a few times if you decide to build your own drop shipping business.

You'll run into suppliers who don't have great inventory management and who do run out of stock, and that will lead to lost sales.

Increased Risk of Competition

The last thing that I could really think of as a negative with drop shipping is the increased risk of competition. If you create your own brand to sell online– let's go back to that chandelier niche– and you make 'Anton Chandeliers'. No one else can go out and create 'Anton Chandeliers'. That's your company and your brand.

When we're drop shipping, we're selling other people's brands who are looking for retailers. And other competitors will likely come across the same supplier and become retailers as well.

So it's competitive, but if it wasn't competitive, it would mean there wasn't money to be made. It would mean there isn't a market for that niche, and it's probably a bad niche to enter.

Frequently Asked Questions

What is drop shipping?

Drop shipping is a retail method where you don't keep products in stock. Instead, you partner with a supplier that stocks its own inventory. You transfer customer orders and shipment details to them, and the supplier ships the order directly to the customer.

Do I have to handle shipping and returns?

You DO NOT handle shipping and returns as a drop shipper. This is the magic of the drop shipping model. Here's why:

1. The supplier's shipping method is already optimized for efficiency and accuracy.

2. Since your suppliers are shipping items in bulk, they get cheaper shipping rates.

3. If the item gets lost or damaged, it's on the supplier's dime.

4. For returns, the supplier usually deals with the customer. You don't have to.

Shouldn't I see the product in person before I sell it?

This actually isn't necessary. If you do proper research beforehand, you should end up picking **quality** products that offer **value**. You can find out if a product is suitable for sale in a few ways:

1. Look at Google, blogs, and retail sites for customer reviews.

2. Find video reviews on YouTube and other sites. Observe the 'unboxing' of the product and gauge the user's reaction to the product.

3. Go to trade shows to see physical versions of the product.

Do I have to list my phone number on my site?

The short answer is yes. In my experience, I can say that adding a real phone number to your site and answering calls is one of the best ways to increase sales.

Do I have to know how to code to build and run a great looking eCommerce store?

Not at all! Sure, it's nice to know a bit about web optimization and design, but Shopify, the platform I recommend with drop shipping, is incredibly user friendly. Along with beautiful pre-made themes, apps, and the customer service support, there's no need to learn any code to start.

Why Shopify? Why not drop ship with Amazon, WooCommerce, or any other platform?

Shopify works… it works *very* well. The customer service is great. It's easy to customize and build a beautiful store. Best of all, it only costs $29 a month to get started.

Why only sell high-ticket products?

I recommend only selling high-ticket products for a few reasons:

1. You make more money per sale.

2. These items are just as easy as cheap products to import to your products page and sell.

3. They are high-quality products that get less returns and happier customers.

How long will it take to create my store?

If you go through my method, this can take anywhere from a week to a couple of months. Savvy web designers or experienced drop shippers could knock out a store in a week. Folks who are new at this may take a bit longer. But don't worry — as long as you stick to the course, you'll be on the right track.

Do I have to know anything about marketing and SEO before I build a drop shipping store?

There are certain techniques for marketing that I'll share later in this book. If you're curious for more, take a gander at our courses, or dig in to our blog! Our site is loaded with eCommerce and marketing goodies!

Do I need to live in the country that my suppliers are in?

This is my favorite question to answer... NO! As long as you have an internet connection, you can drop ship. Just know that if you don't have a United States Bank account, you won't be able to get certain United States based suppliers. The same goes for other countries. I cover this more in my *Doing Business Abroad* course.

Should I drop ship products from China?

I don't recommend it. My method isn't about working with Alibaba and shipping cheap products from China. I encourage you to ship expensive, high quality products that are shipped domestically (or in the US if you can manage it).

PART 2
THE METHOD

Will I Be Successful with Drop Shipping?

You just learned about the basic drop shipping model. You now get the gist of what we teach at Drop Ship Lifestyle, and it's probably apparent that starting a drop shipping business is something *you* could do.

However, before you start a store, there are a few very important questions that you're probably asking:

Will I be successful with drop shipping?

How much money can I expect to make?

How long will I have to wait to see my first sale?

When people come to Drop Ship Lifestyle, they usually want two things: more time and more money

This makes sense, right? Most of us want more money without sacrificing the majority of our priceless time. Creating a *semi-*

automated lifestyle business **is the core** of Drop Ship Lifestyle. It's why I started the program.

I'm going to cover these important questions. I'm also going to cover what you can expect with your drop shipping store; from your potential earnings, to the time it takes you to make your first sale!

I can't make income claims. I can't tell you that you will make $XX amount a day. I can't promise that you'll make a single cent.

First… How much you make with drop shipping depends on *quite a few* variables. One of them being your niche selection; another variable being the time you spend building and managing your business.

When you read about examples I give from successful Drop Ship Lifestyle members, you must understand that these examples are simply *their experiences* in the drop shipping business.

You could meet the same success. You could also fall short of other members' successes. We will cover this in more detail throughout the book.

Second… One of the most important factors when starting your own drop shipping business is your personality. Mindset, personality, goals, and your lifestyle all play a large part in your drop shipping success. Personality and drive also determine how much money you will make.

Getting started in drop shipping isn't hard. I believe anyone can do it. The drop shipping model is proven to work. Don't be afraid to take huge risks and bet it all on yourself. You can't be afraid to fall. Even if you fail, your worse case scenario probably isn't all that bad. However, going above and beyond - making six figures a year - requires a certain type of drive and a certain type of planning.

Is Drop Shipping Worth It?

Let's take a closer look with some real life examples of drop shipping success. These stories answer the question, "Is drop shipping worth it?"

Seeing how REAL people navigate their drop shipping businesses is key to success. Moms, dads, entrepreneurs, travelers, people from all walks of life, have found success through Drop Ship Lifestyle. Here are a few stories from our members.

A Story from Super Mom and Drop Ship Lifestyle Member - Carla S.

Here's a little perspective from a drop shipping member named Carla. She's a mom with a mission who worked hard and grew her business.

"I just wanted to share my little journey. My site launched in September, and last night I hit $10k in sales. I have three very young kids and we have all been hit with lots of colds, flus and viruses in the past few months.

"I have worked really hard and I know I have still got so much to do. I am not tech savvy, and a lot of the small things took me weeks to figure out, but thanks to the support around me, in here and a few other groups. This can be done."

Carla posted this to our private Facebook group in October. By May, she was doing $100k in sales a *month*. Before taking the Drop Ship Lifestyle courses, Carla sold cookie cutters on eBay.

Her margins were low, and the revenue wasn't that great - even though she was selling *a ton* of products. But once she found my method and built her own drop shipping store, things started to change.

She was able to manage a $100k store from her office (aka her living room sofa) and take care of her three young children. Using Google Ads, Facebook remarketing, and other techniques, Carla is able to run a semi-automated drop shipping store and take care of her family. Carla says that "If I can do it, anyone can."

A Story from Entrepreneur Nomad and Drop Ship Lifestyle Member - Johnny FD

Johnny didn't have $1,000 in his bank account several years ago. Now he's retired and on his way to becoming a millionaire. Johnny wrote this on the Drop Ship Lifestyle blog he wrote for us a while back. It's truly reflective of passion for helping people scale up and spend wisely.

> "When I first started my drop shipping store it took me exactly two months before I made a single penny. It was hard to get up every morning and put 6-8 hours of work in on my store without knowing if it would ever amount to anything.

> "But the good news is, if you can get over the hump and earn your first dollar, you can scale it from there. If you can make $1,000 a month online, you can scale that into $100,000 a year."

When Johnny was only making $1,000 a month drop shipping, he realized that he could invest these earnings. He realized that the money he was spending on drop shipping courses and his Shopify subscription were actually *making him money.*

Instead of living the extravagant lifestyle, he pinched pennies and only spent his money where it mattered - even when his drop shipping stores became extremely successful.

Now, he's retired and holds most of his drop shipping earnings in Vanguard index funds such as VTI and small cap value funds such as VBR. Johnny is as savvy as entrepreneurs come.

A Story from Husband / Ex-Nine-to-Fiver and Drop Ship Lifestyle Member - Zach V.

Zach was working the standard nine to five. He wanted freedom. After he visited Thailand for the first time, he knew that something needed to change — he felt a freedom that he never felt before.

> **"That is the beauty of this model... If you want to make $2K a month and live comfortably as a digital nomad in Southeast Asia, you can do that.**
>
> **"If you want to build a big business that can scale to $1M, $5M, $10M+ annually, with an office full of employees and a warehouse, you can do that as well. I truly believe that with drop shipping, the sky's the limit.**
>
> **"If you dream of leaving your job and haven't read *The Four Hour Work* Week by Tim Ferris, I recommend you buy it and read it now. Right when I started to feel myself get a little bit comfortable at my job, I bought and read this book. Immediately, I put together my plan to quit in six months. For me, there were a ton of key takeaways that helped build the foundation for my mindset."**

That's right. Zach quit his job and pursued his dream of owning his own business, choosing his own hours, and traveling when he wanted to travel.

So Zach buckled down, and in less than a year of working with the Drop Ship Lifestyle method, he hit $1 million in sales.

Zach and his wife are now back in Thailand where his dream started. He's focused on scaling his business and growing as an entrepreneur.

What is Your "Why"?

Before you get serious about building your drop shipping business, you have to figure out your "why". Some call it their "mission statement", but I'm talking about what it is that drives you to pursue freedom through an online business.

Listing the things that have always been important to you (family, travel, etc) is a great way to identify your "WHY". Step back and ask yourself these questions:

What does a great day look like to you?

_____

_____

What does real success feel like for you?

_____

_____

Finally, WHY do you want to build a drop shipping store?

_____

_____

How much money do you want to earn monthly with your online store?

_____

How much time (on a weekly basis) are you going to put in to building your business?

_____

How Much Money Can I Expect to Make with Drop Shipping?

Like I said earlier, this largely depends on you. It depends on how much time you put into your store, what products you sell, and how you do business in general.

Before we dive into specific examples of drop shipping revenue, here are some general rules concerning what you can expect to make when drop shipping using my method:

- The average profit margins for Drop Ship Lifestyle's method of drop shipping are around 20%.

- If you sell **high-ticket** items, you will make more than if you were to sell **low-ticket** items.

- If you are smart with how you place your ads, your ad spend won't break the bank… and you'll have many, many more sales.

- If you pick the right niche, you will make more sales, have repeat customers, and you'll have less returns.

- Don't rush the niche selection process. If you do, your chances of drop shipping success could be compromised.

Yes, the list above is vague. Let's go into further detail below. Each of the points are important to remember when starting your store.

How Long Will I Have to Wait Until My First Sale?

I get this question a lot, and for good reason! You don't want your new business to take months to get off the ground. The wait for your first sale kind of depends on your experience in eCommerce.

For me or for someone experienced in drop shipping, I'd estimate one to two *weeks* for the first sale. There are some new Drop Ship Lifestyle members that make their first sale in only one week!

If you're new at all of this, I would expect your first sale to take one to two *months*. So if you're like me, coming into this with lots of eCommerce experience and you:

- are confident when you contact suppliers…

- know what to say to potential suppliers…

- know how to build a demo drop shipping store before you contact suppliers…

- know how to set up traffic…

… Then you could make your first sale in less than two weeks. Otherwise, just be patient knowing it may take a couple of months to make a sale. The time it takes to start making sales depends on a few factors.

1. **How closely you follow my coaching program:** my Drop Ship Blueprint walks you through the entire process for setting up a profitable store. If you follow my program, your chances of success go up. Why? Because I've been

doing this for over a decade. I've had large successes and large failures. I know how to navigate this business.

2. **Your previous technical experience:** if you're keen on web design, or if you're used to pumping out drop shipping stores, getting your store set up and making that first sale can be a breeze.

3. **Your niche selection:** if you choose a good niche, you're going to make sales quicker than if you were to sell in a less optimal niche. Plain and simple.

What are the Profits per Sale?

We are looking at a 25% average profit margin when drop shipping. However, this varies. I've had margins as high as 50% and as low as 15%. It all depends on your supplier and your niche.

The lowest margin I recommend is 15%. This can be too low for some niches, but it can definitely be profitable. *"But Anton,"* you ask. *"People who keep their own inventory make 50% margins."*

This is true. If you rent out warehouse space, ship out products yourself, and handle returns, your profit margins will be higher.

The margins with drop shipping are lower because this way of doing business is fairly hands off. All you do as a drop shipper is get approved by suppliers and make the sale. The supplier does everything else! If you keep inventory, your business is no longer location independent. When you market and drop ship products, you can do it from *anywhere*.

The profit margin tradeoff is a no-brainer in my opinion. The lower profit margins are also one of the main reasons I suggest selling high-ticket products.

Drop Shipping High-Ticket vs Low-Ticket Products

Scenario 1: Low-Ticket Drop Shipping

Take a look at the *Low Cost Items* column on below. As you can see, we are selling this item for $10 retail. The customer goes to your website and purchases your product for $10.

There's a pretty good chance that you'll pay your supplier $5 for the item, and your shipping cost will be somewhere around $3. So what are you left with? $3.

In this scenario, your profit per sale is $2, and that's ONLY if you didn't spend money on advertising. Low-ticket niches like this can be found on websites like Oberlo. It's not what I teach in my program, and it's not something I'd ever recommend.

Scenario 2: High-Ticket Drop Shipping

Here, we are selling an item that sells for $1,000 retail. You sell an item for $1,000 and the item costs you $500 wholesale. Depending on the product size and weight, you can expect to spend $200 on shipping. So you're left with $300 after everything is said and done. Even if you have some ad spend costs, you walk away with a decent chunk of cash.

So my point here? Selling these high and low-ticket products require the same amount of work. The drop shipping process for both of these items is the same:

- You uploaded the **same amount** of products to your website.

- You send the **same traffic** to it.

- You receive the **same orders**.

- You process the orders the **same way** on your end.

But here's the big difference: **the high-ticket drop shipping**

	SCENARIO 1	SCENARIO 2
	LOW TICKET	**HIGH TICKET**
SUPPLIER CHARGES YOU	$5	$500
YOU CHARGE CUSTOMERS	$10	$1000
SHIPPING COSTS	$2	$200
PROFIT	$3	$300

model made 100x the amount of money than the low-ticket model. This scenario gives you an idea of *realistic results* with the *right* drop ship suppliers and the *right* niche price points.

I only sell high-ticket items. This is what I teach at Drop Ship Lifestyle. I've never sold low-ticket items. I only recommend selling in high-ticket niches, and I only work with legitimate suppliers.

So we get how the drop ship model works, and we are getting an idea of how to be successful and make money. But, where will we sell our products? What products will we even sell? Let's get into it!

Where Will I Sell My Products?

One of the first steps in starting a drop shipping store is to decide on where you will be selling your products. There are many choices. Some work and some don't. As far as platforms for drop shipping go, the most popular are Amazon, eBay, and building your own eCommerce store on a platform such as Shopify.

Amazon

One drop shipping option is Amazon. Personally, I don't drop ship on Amazon. However, I do know quite a bit of people who do it successfully.

What I'll say about drop shipping on Amazon is that it's risky. The window for selling products could shrink fast, and you could very likely get wiped out by an over-saturation of competition. On Amazon, making a lot of sales comes down to who has the best price. Furthermore, there's a lot of drop ship suppliers that won't even let you sell on Amazon.

I do have one piece of advice for drop shipping on Amazon: don't put all your eggs in one basket. It's quite common that overnight, a bigger player steps in and starts competing with you. But I can't fully recommend drop shipping on Amazon, especially not as your primary source of income.

Though if your store is up and doing well, and you're looking to scale your business, then Amazon is an okay option for an additional source of income. Still, just my opinion, but you shouldn't rely on all of your income coming from Amazon.

Here's a recap of the reasons why I find drop shipping on Amazon too risky to rely on 100 percent:

1. Not easily scalable.

2. You don't own your customers.

3. You can get wiped out easily.

eBay

Let's talk about why eBay shouldn't even be an option for drop shipping. First of all, the really good suppliers with great brands aren't going to allow eBay drop shipping.

Whenever you sign on and get approved with a new drop ship supplier, your contract will usually state that you're not able to sell on auction websites.

Obviously, that includes eBay, mainly because it dilutes the value of a brand. Good drop ship suppliers, the ones you want to work with, are those who truly care about the value of their brand.

Great suppliers are not going to approve people only to have them jump on eBay and start selling their products at 'auction'.

Just think about a high level company like Gucci. They're not going to approve a seller and say: "Okay, yeah. You can sell these real Gucci bags on eBay. It's fine."

That's not how it works with any good supplier, no matter what the price point of their products or the level of their supplier tier. When it comes to using eBay for drop shipping, don't even think about it.

Here's a recap of the reasons why I never recommend drop shipping on eBay:

1. Potential for *ridiculously low* profit margins.

2. A little thing called customer payment holding. You don't get your hard earned money until way later in the process.

3. Wrong audience. eBay is where people want cheap prices.

Building Your Own Store

The third option is to have your own eCommerce store. This is the drop shipping model that I teach people to follow in my course, and it is what I always recommend.

Here are four of the biggest benefits to putting in the effort to build your own online store.

1. This store is YOURS. It's a real asset that you can actually sell if you decided to.

2. You have more choices for traffic sources.

3. You own the customer and the data.

4. You can implement the changes your market wants.

Benefit #1: You're Not Competing Solely on Price

First, you're not competing solely on the price of an item. When you own your own drop shipping business, you own that platform and data. It's no longer only about price.

Sure, people can find your products elsewhere, but when they're visiting your eCommerce store, they're not seeing all of your competitors like they do on eBay and Amazon.

They're seeing your store and *your store only* when making buying decisions. The same can't be said for drop shipping on Amazon or eBay alone.

Benefit #2: You Have More Choices for Additional Traffic Sources

When you own your own drop shipping store, you have more traffic sources available to you. When you're drop shipping on eBay or Amazon, your store's traffic is Amazon and eBay's traffic. Some people see that as a benefit to drop shipping on those platforms, but I see it as limiting.

In my opinion, what makes owning your own drop shipping store better is having access to certain advertising options that you just don't get with Amazon or eBay.

That's something that I'm not going to go into much detail about now, because the possibilities with paid traffic is a whole other section in this book.

Benefit #3: You Own the Customer and the Data

The next benefit of owning your own eCommerce store is having the customer's data. This is a huge drawback on Amazon, where you don't even get your customer's email address! When someone buys from you on Amazon, you'll ship them the product, but you won't know who that person is.

When you have your own eCommerce store, you own all of this data. When these customers buy from you, you gain:

- Names

- Addresses

- Phone Numbers

- But most importantly, you have your customers' email addresses

And that leads into the next benefit of owning your own store. If you have your customer's information, especially their email address, you can extend the lifetime value of your customer.

This lets you follow up sales with upsells and add ons via automated email. You could also send customers holiday promo campaigns, and any other promotional emails they might be interested in.

Benefit #4: You Can Implement the Changes Your Market Wants

The next benefit of having your own store is that you can implement the changes that your market wants. That means you're able to target specific buyers.

On sites like eBay or Amazon, they're not targeting one specific customer because they sell everything. They are targeting anyone who could purchase anything from them.

When you have your own drop shipping store, you can make it super specific, targeting an exact buying demographic. Find out who your ideal customer is and make your drop shipping store revolve around them.

Making your drop ship store highly targeted will greatly increase your conversion rate when you compare your site to eBay or Amazon.

Now, you can start to understand why I'm such a big fan of starting and selling from your own eCommerce store. Just remember, you should never sell on eBay, and you shouldn't start your drop shipping career on Amazon.

For You, What are the Pros & Cons of Starting a Drop Shipping Business?

PROS:

_____

_____

_____

CONS:

_____

_____

_____

Where to Build Your Drop Shipping Store

So how do you go about building your drop shipping store? Well, these site builders are the five most popular tools for building your store. While there are more out there, these are the four you will hear about most.

WordPress

The first is WordPress, and you might already be familiar with this platform. Maybe you've built a blog on this platform before.

Either way, I'm sure you've been to a WordPress sites many times. They power around 60% of all websites online. WooCommerce is a plugin for WordPress that allows you to build an eCommerce store on the WordPress platform.

Now the problem with WordPress is that it's self hosted. That means that you need to pay for a server somewhere. You have to upload WordPress and WooCommerce, and then you're responsible for the security. What kind of security? Basically, you'll need web security to keep hackers off of your eCommerce website.

It's also important to note if something breaks on your drop ship site, it's up to you to get fixed. You either do this yourself or pay someone to fix it for you.

If there's a problem with your self-hosted WordPress site, no one's going to just jump in there and fix it for you for free. You host it, you control it. That's how WordPress and WooCommerce work.

Magento

Magento is a great eCommerce platform. However, it's for very advanced internet retailers. Generally, the price isn't worth it for 99% of us drop shippers.

I don't use Magneto now, but I have in the past with other drop shipping stores. But for niche specific stores– the ones I teach people to build in my drop shipping course, they don't need that kind of power. This platform is far too expensive and even harder to customize, so it's not worth it for what we need.

BigCommerce

The next option would be BigCommerce, which is a hosted eCommerce platform. A hosted eCommerce platform is one that hosts your drop shipping store for you.

They make sure your eCommerce store is secure and safe from hackers. More importantly, they make sure that your customers' information is safe. And if anything breaks, the BigCommerce team will fix it for you.

Now, I do like BigCommerce but I have one problem: their customer service. When I've used them in the past, I had some issues and found their customer service to be sub par.

Shopify

That leaves us at the last option: Shopify. They've been around since 2004, and they're now one of the biggest eCommerce platforms. And simply put, they are amazing for drop shipping. You could easily build an incredibly gorgeous drop ship store with them.

Drop ship stores built using Shopify are super easy to control and extremely secure. Plus, their customer support is available 24/7 and they never hesitate to jump on a call or live chat to help you out. They are more than happy to fix your store or take care of payment processing!

What's great about Shopify is their massive app store. This store has hundreds of Shopify apps that let you completely control how your store looks and functions.

When it comes to pricing, Shopify steals the show. Their plans start at a very low $29 a month. If you don't like paying monthly fees, remember everything they're offering for that cost. When you're trying to build a business, spending $29 in overhead once a month should not be a concern.

So to recap... As for building a drop shipping store with **WooCommerce**, I wouldn't because of security issues. The risk just isn't worth it. I'd rather pay $29 a month on Shopify just for peace of mind.

There's **Magento**. This is for the massive drop shipping stores and something we don't need. And while **BigCommerce** is a good option for drop shipping, customer support is not great and can cause more headaches.

This just leaves **Shopify**. And hands down, it's the winning platform for me. For now, I wouldn't recommend any other platform.

What Products Should I Sell?

According to Google, a niche is a nook or cranny, a vocation or calling, or **a specialized segment of the market for a particular kind of product or service.**

That last definition is what we focus on in this book. "Niche selection" is one of the first terms you'll see when researching selling online. You'll hear folks say things like "Niche selection is everything," and "A successful store starts with a great niche."

And listen close, because the folks that value their niches are the ones who build successful drop shipping stores. Niche selection is vital to your drop shipping business' success. There's a reason why drop shippers are completely obsessed with niches.

Choosing a Niche for Drop Shipping

When you are choosing a niche, you're choosing products that exist within a **specific market.** These products are exclusive and specific to a *small portion* of the entire online market (e.g., a site that sells straight razors **vs** Amazon).

You don't want to build a shopping mall-type site (like Amazon), where you sell potted plants, computer screens, wallpaper, and everything in between. Shopping mall stores like Amazon are NOT niche specific. Niche specific stores address a specific market segment.

For example, if I wanted to sell high-end pet products, that's what my store would sell: HIGH-END PET PRODUCTS. Not high-end pet products AND coffee AND ceramics AND whatever else…

We'll be covering this throughout the book, but let's go through some reasons why choosing a niche so important:

- Niche markets make more conversions than non-niche markets.

- Specific niches attract buyer traffic. This means less of your money is put into ad spend, and more money is made on sales.

- Selling into the right niche market lets you, the small business owner, actually make sales and compete! There's no way you can compete with Amazon. Niche eCommerce stores allow you to truly target your niche market.

- Choosing a single niche to target gives you specific data about your audience. This data is priceless. If you're targeting 10 different niches on your store, getting relevant information about the buying habits of your audience can be difficult. Selling in a specific niche really lets you hone in your marketing focus. You're selling specific products to a specific audience.

I'm going to walk through all of this information in detail throughout this portion of the book, but know one thing before you continue on: DON'T RUSH THROUGH THE NICHE SELECTION PROCESS. This isn't a spot where you want to try saving time.

If there is *one thing* you don't want to rush, it's niche selection. Like I said before, my method of drop shipping lets you run your store in 30 minutes a day or less. But...

In the beginning, it takes a bit of work to build your store. For the newcomer, this can take anywhere from 40 to 60 hours — or longer. I focus on building a *really* strong foundation before launching a drop shipping store. Much of this time is spent on niche selection. It's always smart to put a good amount of research into the niche you'll be selling in.

Niche Selection Criteria

Before we actually move on to pick a niche, there are some criteria that will help you find something that's profitable. After being in eCommerce for more than a decade, you pick up some things. I've done it the hard way, and I've also done niche selection the easy way.

I stick to these rules because over the past 10 years, I found that they helped me create a solid foundation. We'll dive into each of these criteria individually but a good niche will be three things:

- It will fall into our target price range of at least $200.

- It will appeal to the upper-middle class.

- Something that consumers will have no brand loyalty to.

Criteria #1: Pricing

The products that you sell should at least be sold for $200 or more. Why?

1. You'll spend the same amount of time processing a $20 order as you would a $2,000 order. If you're going to be doing the work, you might as well have a chance of making some real money on each sale. This brings us to my next point.

2. Using my method of drop shipping, your average profit margin will be around 25% of the gross revenue. This means that each $2,000 sale would yield a profit of around $500. This would also mean that each $20 sale yields a profit of approximately $5... If both the $20 product and the $2,000 product are just as easy to sell, your decision of which product to feature on your store should be a no brainer.

3. It is important to note that although I do have websites that sell products for $999 and up, I have noticed that many customers call in when placing orders at that price range. If you are comfortable on the phone, then this shouldn't be a problem. However, if you want to run an online store where the majority of orders are made online, I recommend selling items priced between $200 and $1000.

Criteria #2: Target Market

I've sold products online that appeal to the wealthy, products that appeal to the middle class, and products that appeal to lower income households. From my experience, I found that it is most effective to target the upper-middle class.

The upper-middle class is made up of online shoppers who have household incomes of $100,000 or more. If you sell products that appeal to low income or high income households, you'll have a lot more work to do. Trust me on this.

After spending all these years selling products online, I've come to realize that low income household products require MUCH more pre-selling, way more interaction with the customers, and a deluge of complaints and returns. The same can be said about selling to high income households. These folks expect more personalized service and require much more effort to close the sale.

Drop shipping is a business model that requires very little effort to run. This book outlines a method where you can put forth the smallest amount of effort while generating the largest amount of sales possible. Your time is valuable, so we want to make the most out of the time you do spend running your store.

We are looking to sell to individuals and families with disposable incomes. These upper-middle class individuals are used to shopping online, and therefore, are comfortable making large purchases over the internet.

Criteria #3: The Brand Loyalty Problem

What kind of computer or cell phone do you have? Is it the same brand as your last computer? Chances are if you own a Mac, the next computer you buy will also be a Mac. Why? Brand loyalty. When selling online, you want to avoid selling products that have brand loyalty.

For example, I would not try to sell TVs online. Most customers who are buying a TV engage in a ton of research. They want to find which TV is best for them, or they wish to purchase the same brand of TV they owned in the past.

These people already researched which TV brand has the best picture quality, warranty, and the best reviews online. If I wanted to sell TVs that people are actually buying (Sony, Panasonic, LG, etc.) there is no way I would be able to compete with brick and mortar companies. My small drop shipping store would never get the same payment and pricing terms as Best Buy or any of the big box stores.

So, what type of products should you sell? Look for products that customers are thinking about buying… but they don't know which brand they should buy. We need to look for products that customers would be comfortable buying from ANY brand.

Examples of Drop Shipping Store Customers

Example #1: Joan

Joan lives on a lake, and she decides that she wants to start stand-up paddle boarding. She needs a paddle board and a paddle, but she has no prior knowledge of this sport or what brands are well known. Joan couldn't care less about which company makes the board — as long as she can find some good reviews on products that sit at the right price.

Paddle boarding is a fantastic example of a viable niche. The average cost of a stand-up paddle board and paddle is over $700.

The average customer does not care what brand they are buying, and the sport is likely to appeal to those who purchase these items with their disposable income (the upper-middle class).

Example #2: Mr. and Mrs. Smith

Mr. and Mrs. Smith just moved into a new home. There's an enormous chandelier hanging in the entryway, and they can't stand it. The couple takes a trip to the local Home Depot & Lowe's to find a replacement, but they can't find anything that they both agree on.

They know what style chandelier they wish to buy, but it's not available locally. Mrs. Smith goes online and searches for a 30" x 30" entryway chandelier, and she finds an online store with hundreds of options. Here, she finds exactly what she wants.

This is another great example of a product to sell online. Chandeliers are expensive, they appeal to the upper-middle class, and the average customer doesn't care what brand they're buying as long as they like what they see.

Niche Selection Brainstorm

On the these two pages, take some time to think of products to drop ship based on my criteria. Set a timer for 20 minutes and jot down as many product niches as you can. We will go back to this list in the next section.

Here are some questions to help you start brainstorming:

- What do people like to do on vacation?

- What are the hobbies of your family and friends?

- What's the most expensive item in the room right now?

Niche Selection Methods

To provide some background, my very first high-ticket eCommerce store started making money within 24 hours of going live. I made a $485 sale the first night that my store was able to accept orders.

I'm not telling you this to show off. I'm telling you because I want you to know the secret to my drop shipping method– the same secret I used to make another $3,000 in sales those first three weeks.

People are often shocked when they hear this story. It sounds like I just threw together an online shop and starting making money through luck… but the truth is that I spent A LOT of time researching prior to launching. Again, it's all about preparation.

Before my first high-ticket online store went live, which was back in 2007, I did a ton of market research in order to have the best chance of success come launch time.

There was one reason that I made $485 within hours of launching. It was because I found a profitable niche that fit a certain criteria.

Below are a few methods that you need to know in order to select profitable drop shipping products. These methods will help you on the path to finding a profitable niche.

Method #1: Focused Brainstorming

Put on your thinking cap. It's time to come up with some niches. Hopefully you already came up with some during the action task in the last section. If you're stuck, no worries. I have some tips that will point you in the right direction.

To brainstorm new ideas, I often think of things I recently bought online. I also ask my family and friends about any recent purchases they've made. Think about what you've bought in the past.

List the last five items you or family/friends have purchased online:

1. _____

2. _____

3. _____

4. _____

5. _____

Think about all your family and friends and what they have in their houses or what hobbies they partake in. Think about the furniture and equipment in the cafe that you're reading this book in right now!

I write everything down... even if it seems questionable at the time. I take my list and begin running my brainstormed niches through some tests. You'll find that there are plenty of profitable niches, but this doesn't mean you should rush into each and every one.

Action Task

Add to the niche brainstorming list that you started in the last section. I want you to come up with 50 niches total. I think you'll find that this isn't as daunting as it once was. You should do this before you move forward.

5 Things to Consider with Your Niche

1. **COMPETITION** - Scout out other drop shipping stores and see what products are over-saturated. You don't want to sell those.

2. **LOYALTY** - Don't go for a niche or product that is dominated by any national brand(s).

3. **PRICING** - The higher the price of the product, the greater your revenue will be!

4. **WEIGHT** - Shipping is expensive. A winning combo as a drop shipper is a high-priced product that has low shipping weights.

5. **RETURNS** - Don't pick a product with sizing and style preferences. These will have an absurd return rate.

Method #2: Research and Evaluate Current Drop Shipping Trends

Go to Google Shopping and start typing in niches from your list of 50 niche ideas. Now, go to the stores you find online and browse around. Some of the stores you visit will be drop shippers, and some of the stores will be brick and mortar stores' internet sites.

To See if a Store is Drop Shipping...

Go to their **About Us** and **Contact** pages. If you see actual store locations, not a PO box or office addresses, then it's likely that you're not looking at a drop shipping store. Also, look and see how the store ships their products. If they explain that they don't actually ship the products they sell, then you can rest assured they are probably drop shipping.

Find as many drop shippers as you can. Observe what products they sell and how they do business. Look at which products are flying like hot cakes and which ones the industry stays away from.

Looking at Your Competitors' Suppliers

Your drop shipping competitors will have a list of suppliers on their website. These lists are a free resource to you. They tell you how many drop shipping suppliers exist in your niche.

Find the drop shipping stores in your niche, count all of the different suppliers, and make sure that there are *at least 20 suppliers* you can potentially work with.

If there are less than 20 suppliers in your prospective niche, move on to the next niche idea.

Things Change

In the early 2000's, when I first started in eCommerce, I wasn't drop shipping. I was importing from China. I contacted a few suppliers that I had found on Alibaba and requested price lists for these exact products.

I then contacted a customs broker and got shipping quotes for a container of the products. Next, I factored in all of my other expenses and learned I could sell these on eBay at the same price as many competitors and make a 50%+ profit on each sale! But that was back in 2007…

Things have changed over the years, and I highly recommend not working on eBay. I discussed this in Part 1 of this book. Exclusively searching for drop shipping trends on Amazon and eBay will lead you astray. Broaden up your horizons and do your own research.

Method #3: Think Like a Marketer

The first, and most important, tip I will share on finding a profitable drop shipping niche is to SELL EXPENSIVE ITEMS! Based on my experience, the average net profit when drop shipping is about 25% of your total sales.

You'll make around 25% profit on selling both $1,000 items and $10 items... Which means that you could either make **$2050** (25% of $1,000) or **$2.50** (25% of $10) per sale. As you can see, if you want to make money, you *need* to sell expensive items. Not that complicated, right?

Sure, there are folks that have made decent money selling cheap items like iPhone cases, but it's tough. It's more difficult to make a sustainable income selling cheap items than with expensive, high-ticket products.

Once you've made sure that your niche products are expensive enough (products that are at least $200), you need to find out if the suppliers of products in your niche enforce MAP policies.

If your Google search results (from Method #2) show a bunch of different prices that are all over the place, then the particular supplier of that product does NOT enforce MAP.

On the other hand, if the results say something like "$999 from three stores" and there are no other prices listed for the same exact item, then you've likely found a supplier that enforces MAP.

Do I Need to Know a lot About My Niche to Sell in it?

The answer is no. You need to find niches that are profitable–not niches that you know a lot about. Sure, it may help if you're a bit knowledgeable of your niche, but that knowledge will come over time.

If for some reason you can't answer a customer's question about a particular product, you can always call your supplier to get the answer.

You don't need to become an expert in your niche. All you need to do is research whether or not customers are looking to buy. We want to sell awesome products to awesome customers. Niche selection is how we do this.

To learn more about the products you sell, you can always:

- Watch YouTube 'unboxings'

- Read product reviews

- Go to trade shows.

See? No sweat! This method of research has always worked for me. To conclude the niche selection portion of the book…Be smart and keep it simple. Remember that as the retailer, all you pay is the wholesale cost of the product and shipping.

If you can find products to sell that are relatively light AND expensive, you'll probably pay less in shipping. This means that your revenue could potentially be higher.

I'm not saying to only sell light items. Heavy items can indeed be profitable. What I'm saying is that every little detail matters when choosing a niche.

3X Your Niche List

Here are three techniques you can use to find even more niches based on the ones listed in the Method #1 section above (or based on your niche list)!.

Niching Down

This is when you go from a broader niche category to a more specific category. For instance, if you want to sell "camping equipment" but are finding that market to be oversaturated, you could niche down and focus on a **specific element of the broader niche**, such as sleeping bags.

Niching Up

This is the opposite of niching down. You might use the niching up technique if you've found a good niche that doesn't have as many suppliers or as much search volume as you would like to see.

For instance, if you want to sell pottery wheels but **there are not enough suppliers or demand**, you may niche up and choose to sell pottery equipment. This would also include kilns, brushes, etc…

Niching Sideways

This is a technique that you can use to find multiple, similar niches to then start up two or more related eCommerce stores that can cross promote one another. Taking from the example above, let's say you found that pottery wheels had enough suppliers and a good search volume.

You capitalize and make a successful eCommerce store out of this niche. This is when it may be a good idea to niche sideways and start a pottery kilns eCommerce store, which you could **cross promote** with your existing store.

Testing Your Niche

I want to go over four free tools that I use when making sure there's money in a niche. You've most likely heard or used some of these tools. However, you've probably never used these tools in the ways I'm about to show you.

NOTE: I do each of these tests in order. If the niche fails the first test, I scrap it immediately and move on to research another niche.

Tool #1: Google Keyword Planner

If you know anything about online marketing, you're probably familiar with this tool. If not, know that it's easy to use, and free!

Find the Keyword Planner at https://adwords.google.com/KeywordPlanner and then Google will walk you through the sign-up process. Once you're inside, click on the box that says *"Get search volume data and trends"*, and enter a top level keyword for your niche.

For instance, if you're selling garden fountains, your keyword would be something like *"water features"*. You don't want to get super specific like *"yard water fountains for homes,"* as there won't be enough search volume.

Next, select the country you are planning on selling in and exclude the rest of the world. When the page loads, click on the tab that says, "Keyword Ideas". You'll see the search volume for your keyword.

If the search volume in your country for your keyword is **more than a ten thousand per month**, move on to the next step! If not, make a note and move on to your next niche.

Tool #2: Google Trends

The next tool we're using is Google Trends. Put in the same keyword that you used in Google Keyword Planner, and see what the results are. If the chart shows the keyword trending down, you probably want to avoid the niche.

For instance, the keyword *"printing press"* is probably trending down more and more, as it becomes a forgotten concept. You would probably not expect a lot of business if you chose to open up an old fashioned printing press...

Another benefit to Google Trends is that you can tell in advance if your niche is seasonal. For example, type in *"water features"*. You will see that it gets a spike in searches every spring, so it is most likely a seasonal niche.

Tool #3: Google Search

Now, go to Google's search feature, which you are probably very familiar with and type in your keyword to see what comes up. Go to Google and search for *"entryway chandelier"*. Observe the ads that come up.

The only reason that advertisers would buy ad space for these ads is if these niches were profitable. The previous two tools proved to us that there was search traffic, but this tool is the first indication that there is money in the niche.

If these products are available, and people are paying money to place these ads, it can be a sign that there is *demand for these products*. If you use Google search and no ads shows up... well, it may be because there is extremely low demand for the product in question.

Tool #4: Wayback Machine

You may not be too familiar with this tool. It's called the Wayback Machine. Before you use this tool, you need to find at least one potential competitor's website. You're going to use Wayback Machine to dig deeper into their website history.

Remember, you can find competitors by searching for your keyword on Google and clicking on the ads. It's important to note that when you're researching your niche, there will probably be two types of stores carrying the item in question:

Type 1: Shopping mall style stores like Amazon.

Type 2: Niche specific stores.

Your competitor will be Type 2. Take your competitor's URL and paste it into the WayBack Machine. This site will allow you to go back and see what changes they made to their website over time.

If your competitor has been in business for a while - **making changes over time** to suite their audience - that's a good sign. When we are deciding on a niche, we are looking for not only initial profitability, but longevity and potential of a niche.

When Researching Your Niche, Don't Forget...

1. **Average Product Price** $200 or more

2. **Buyer Demographics** Upper-middle class

3. **Brand Loyalty** NO brand loyalty

4. **Drop Ship Friendly** Search on Google and explore if your competitors are drop shipping

5. **Quantity of Suppliers** 20 suppliers or more in a niche

How to Find Drop Shipping Suppliers

Let's take a look at how to partner your legitimate eCommerce business with legit suppliers. We aren't going to settle for just anyone. When you work with a supplier, in a sense, you're working with a business partner. The better your store does, the more money your supplier makes. The better quality products your supplier manufactures, the happier your customers will be.

The 4 Step Supplier Research Process

In previous sections, I've covered what type of suppliers you want to stay away from. Which may leave you wondering what kind of suppliers you do want to work with... Here's how I find good drop ship suppliers and get approved to sell their products.

1. Search in Google to see who is selling in your niche.

The first step to finding suppliers lies in an unlikely place: taking a look at your future competitors' websites. We're going to find the top eCommerce websites that are already selling the products in your chosen niche.

For instance, if you've chosen to sell entryway chandeliers. The first step toward finding suppliers is to go to Google and type in your main keyword, "entryway chandelier".

Then, find as many of the online stores relevant to your niche as you can in the first page or two of Google and write down their names in the **Competitors Research Table** located in the back of this book.

2. Head to the websites of your future competitors.

Once you've got a list of online stores relevant to your niche, the next step is to go through and weed out all of the stores that have physical locations or showrooms, leaving ONLY the ones that sell *exclusively* online.

We do this because some product suppliers only work with brick and mortar retailers. These brick-and-mortar locations have internet stores as well, but we aren't competing with them. This is how we weed out brick and mortar only suppliers.

3. Look for a page or section that has either their brands, suppliers, or manufacturers listed.

Find all of the suppliers from the remaining eCommerce stores in your search. This is easy as many websites make their suppliers identifiable. Just go to the first website and look for a section called "Brands" and/or "Manufacturers".

You may need to look in the header, footer, sidebar, or even sitemap to find this. Once you do, you'll find that many stores will end up listing 10, 20, or even 100 brands.

4. Add those companies to a 'Master List' of suppliers.

Building a "Supplier Master List" is a fantastic way to keep track of all of the steps listed above. You'll refer to this list for all future drop ship suppliers in your niche.

Create a "Supplier Name" column in the first column of your spreadsheet, and paste all of the supplier names that you find into this column.

Fill out the details and contact information for each supplier you find. Repeat this for each website and you will quickly find yourself with plenty of suppliers to contact. In most cases — you will quickly find yourself with more suppliers than you need to make a ton of money drop shipping!

Research Your Competitors

After deciding on a solid drop shipping niche to sell in, you'll want to find retailers that are *already* selling products in that niche. Our goal with this is to find our competitors' suppliers.

Every good niche has some competition. There's competition because people are actually making money in these niches. This is why you need to visit your competitors' websites.

We will contact these suppliers and ask if they would like to work with us as well. To do this, use Google and search for your niche.

Go through the top results on Google, and look through these stores. You're trying to find out **who** these stores are selling for.

So there are a few different ways to find your competitors' suppliers. Once you're on your competitors' websites, look for sections that say something similar to:

- "Brands"

- "Manufacturers"

- "Suppliers"

Now, to keep track of these competitors and suppliers, you need to fill out a master list. You're going to contact these suppliers later to try to get them on board with your store. You can fill out the pages below, or create your own digital spreadsheet.

Two Common Supplier Mistakes to Avoid Making

Before you begin contacting suppliers, let's talk about the two types of mistakes to avoid when you're searching for drop ship suppliers. And unfortunately, a lot of new drop shippers make these supplier mistakes.

Supplier Mistake #1: DON'T USE Drop Ship Directories

The suppliers you work with won't charge you for access to their products. Remember, a supplier is kind of like a business partner.

They don't want to make money off of giving you access to a list. They want to make money on you selling their products to happy customers! They are trying to build a brand, and you are trying to build a business selling their products.

Supplier Mistake #2: Buying A Turnkey Drop Shipping Business

If you research drop shipping, you'll find plenty of turnkey drop shipping stores for sale. **Turnkey stores** are 'ready to go' drop shipping stores sold on low-end auction websites. It's a quick way for sellers to make a buck. Usually a huge waste of time and money for the buyer. Turnkey drop shipping stores are full of:

- Drop shipping products that are overpriced and unsellable.

- Traffic sources that everyone else uses and won't work for you, as your prices will be too high.

Don't buy a turnkey store, no matter how tempting it looks, no matter how good the deal is.

The 3 Tiers of Suppliers You Will Want to Work With

Not all drop shipping suppliers are created equal and not all suppliers are disguised as middlemen! Depending on a few key factors, "good" suppliers can fall into one of three tiers: bronze, silver, or gold.

I've separated suppliers into three tiers. These are my personal terms for them, so you won't find suppliers listing themselves as "silver" or "gold".

When starting out, it's very unlikely that you'll be able to work with gold tier suppliers, but you can still make good money working with silver drop shipping suppliers.

As you establish your business and work with more and more suppliers, you'll gain access to gold drop shipping suppliers.

Bronze Suppliers

One of the hallmarks of each tier is the level of exclusivity. If a drop shipping supplier allows anyone who fills out a form to sell for them, then they are likely bronze.

These suppliers aren't brands that want retailers, they are middlemen who make money off of fees they charge you. A few other features of bronze drop shipping suppliers are:

- Allow anyone to sell for them.

- Do not enforce MAP policies.

- Inconsistent product quality.

- Bad customer service.

Silver Suppliers

These are the suppliers that you'll start drop shipping with. They are actual brands looking for retailers to sell their products. Silver suppliers won't work with every person that applies. This means there will be some back and forth before you're approved. Here are a few other characteristics of silver tier drop shipping suppliers:

- Picky about who sells for them.

- Enforces MAP policies.

- Good product quality.

- Good customer service.

Gold Suppliers

After a few months of using silver drop shipping suppliers, you can start reaching out to some of the top tiered, gold suppliers. These are your ideal drop ship suppliers that will make you the most money and reduce your customer service issues.

One of the things that makes a gold drop shipping supplier gold is they only work with *very* few retailers. That's because they are working really hard to create a quality brand and are willing to do a lot more work with their retailers to give the best experience for their customers.

With that in mind, they're very strict with their pricing policies. They will absolutely have MAP pricing and if you break this policy they will stop being your supplier. Here is a recap of what makes a drop shipping supplier gold tiered:

- Very picky about who sells for them.

- Enforces MAP policies.

- Great product quality.

- Great customer service.

Getting Approved by Drop Ship Suppliers

Drop shipping suppliers are looking for retailers that can provide a good buyer experience and exceptional customer service. Since you're representing their brand, they want you to meet the level of their customer service (or better). That way there is a consistent, positive, experience with their brand.

When talking to them, you need to be brand focused and present yourself as a professional. Make sure your responses are friendly and timely, giving them a sample of your customer service through every interaction they have with you.

This also means that you have to build a website before you pick up the phone. It doesn't have to be the best website ever, just professional enough that they can imagine their products being sold there. It has to line up with their brand. This builds trust and credibility.

Your drop shipping suppliers are your partners and they want to work with someone that they can rely on. With your website built, you're already demonstrating your commitment and abilities.

Here are a few secrets for getting approved:

Secret #1: Build a Demo Store

Now that you've picked your niche and researched your drop shipping suppliers, it's time to build your drop shipping store website! You're going to build your store on Shopify **before** you're approved with any suppliers.

Why build a store already? Because no legitimate supplier is going to approve you before they see your drop shipping store. Here's a conversation you DON'T WANT to have with your drop shipping suppliers:

You: *Hey, I want to sell your products!*

Supplier: *Okay, can we see your website?*

You: *Oh, I don't have one.*

Supplier: **Click of the phone hanging up**

That's how you lose potential drop ship suppliers. Without a website they can see, they won't give you the time of the day.

Before you have suppliers, your online storefront is just a 'demo' store. This is so drop ship suppliers can preview your store.

They can click around, but nothing will actually be for sale yet. They will get a feel for how their products will be presented. They want to know if you will properly represent their brand.

This strategy shows suppliers that you're serious, and that if they approve you, you have an actual platform to sell from.

Secret #2: Know How to Explain Marketing Techniques

When you finally reach out to these drop ship suppliers, be prepared to discuss your marketing techniques and how good your customer service is.

You really need to know at least a few marketing tricks before you reach out to potential suppliers. Because again, it's not their job to approve everyone. It's their job to build brands, and they need competent retailers to do that. To learn more about eCommerce marketing, I recommend:

- Going through an online course.

- Watching YouTube videos.

- Working with my online coaching program.

- Googling it! Find articles and read everything you can.

This way, when you're talking to drop ship suppliers and they ask how you're going to market their drop shipping products, you can at least hold a conversation with them.

You don't have to be the biggest marketing expert in the world, but you should understand how eCommerce marketing works.

Secret #3: Customer Service is Everything!

When talking to the drop shipping suppliers, you need to focus on how important customer service is to you. This is often overlooked by retailers, but it's something that means everything to suppliers.

Once suppliers approve you and you're selling for them, you become an authorized retailer promoting their brand. This is why they **only** want to work with people who will treat their customers right. It reflects on their brand… that's a big deal!

Make sure whenever you're having these conversations with your future suppliers that you explain:

- How important customer service is to you and your business.

- That you know how to treat your customers right.

- That their customers will have a pleasant buying experience with your store, encouraging repeat business.

Remember, the goal is for **everyone** to make money. For this to happen, customers have to be the focus. Now that you are ready to get approved with these suppliers, it's time to start contacting them.

How to Contact Suppliers

This is one thing that I receive a lot of questions and concerns about: **calling suppliers**. Sure, it can be scary at first, but it's absolutely worth it.

It is important to note, no matter how long you have been in this business, no matter how nice your website looks, and no matter how much traffic you already have in place, not every supplier you apply with will approve you for an account. So don't get too discouraged when someone doesn't approve you right away.

Know that there are certainly things you can do and say to increase your chances and boost your supplier approval rating. Based on my experience, all drop ship suppliers are looking for certain traits in their retailers.

If you take away anything from this section, remember this: If there is a phone number on the supplier's website, you should call and tell whoever answers the same thing:

- You own/work with [yourwebsite.com],

- You are looking to increase your product catalog by adding their products,

- And you would like to know who to speak to about setting up an eCommerce account.

I go into more detail in my course, but know that this is **vital to your success**. Stick to these three things. Always. If no one is available to talk now, get their e-mail address and/or direct phone number and follow up later. You're going to need to be persistent.

I try to keep my conversations as brief as possible. Here is a typical conversation I have with the supplier's person in charge of eCommerce accounts:

"Hi [account managers name],

My name is Anton and I am the lead buyer for [MyCompany Inc], we currently manage ten different eCommerce stores in various niches and we recently noticed an opportunity in the [suppliers products] niche. We have just launched [newnichewebsite.com] and we are looking for suppliers who are interested in working together.

Based on the market research that we have done my team and I are confident that our marketing techniques will make this new venture our most successful yet.

We are not looking for payment terms, we are just looking to build a solid business relationship. Can you tell me how we can go about applying for an account?"

If the supplier is interested in doing business with you, they will email a few basic forms that you need to complete. They need standard information from you such as your business name, address, phone number, and billing information. OR…

They could also tell you that they are not accepting any new retailers at this time. I always ask them when they will be accepting new applications and make a note in my Supplier Spreadsheet.

Best Practices for Doing Business with Suppliers

Follow Up Regularly

If you want to land a decent supplier, you'll need to follow up regularly. The legitimate suppliers aren't likely to approve you after the first contact. Remember, unlike drop shipping directories, legitimate suppliers aren't looking to approve *as many people as possible.*

These suppliers are building brands. It's important that you sell yourself as an online business having some degree of marketing knowledge and customer service. It's also important to follow up regularly after the first conversation.

Even a veteran drop shipper like myself doesn't get instantly approved with every supplier I contact. At first, they usually say:

- To follow up in a month.

- They're busy.

- They'll get back to me (they never do).

This just means that I have to take initiative and follow up with those drop ship suppliers.

Keep Excellent Notes

It's crucial that you keep excellent notes about every potential supplier you speak to. If they say to call back, make a note of when to call back. If they say they're going to send you something, ask them when they'll send it by and make sure you follow up. It's **your responsibility** to make these supplier approvals happen... not theirs.

Here are a few extra tips for getting approved with suppliers:

- Have a professional email address (I.E., joe@joekayaks.com) from your web domain when contacting suppliers.

- Don't refer to yourself as a drop shipper, but instead an online retailer.

- Think of each drop shipping supplier as a long-term business partner and treat them accordingly.

How Will I Get People to Buy From My Store?

So your demo store is built, you're approved by suppliers, and you're ready to go. How do you get traffic to your drop shipping store?

Before I dive into our traffic sources, I just want to make it very clear how you should approach traffic.

Firstly, you don't need all the traffic in the world. A lot of people who are starting out in eCommerce think that they need thousands of visitors a day to make sales.

But you don't need Amazon level traffic to be successful. Why? Because *you're not trying to compete with everyone.* All you're trying to do is get enough sales to reach the income goals you've set for yourself.

If you want to beat Amazon, I can't help you. However, if you want to build an online business that's profitable, I can definitely help with that.

The Right Type of Traffic

In order to succeed with your drop shipping site, you need buyer traffic. Let's pretend you have a thousand people visiting your drop ship site every day.

That's a great number, but are they looking to buy, or are they just random people who stumbled across your drop shipping site while searching for something online?

There's a huge difference between people looking to buy and people just surfing the web. You don't need a thousand visitors a day to make money. You don't even need a hundred visitors on your drop shipping site a day to make money. Sure, it's ideal, but that metric shouldn't be your *main* focus.

Instead, you should be focused on getting visitors who are ready to buy. For example, let's say you had 10 people come to your drop shipping site every day and those 10 people were buyers.

They found your site, and they'll pay a $1,000 for your drop shipping products. With traffic like that, you could have a very successful drop shipping business.

Whereas, if 100 people a day were to come to your site, but only *five* buy...I think you get the picture. Buyer traffic is good traffic.

Where to Find Buyer Traffic

There are a lot of different ways to find buyers for your drop shipping site. I could spend hours talking about traffic and how I use it with Drop Ship Lifestyle. But for now, I am going to show you some of most common methods of attracting buyers to your drop shipping site.

Traffic Source #1: Google Shopping

If you've ever searched for a physical product on Google, you've likely seen some product images, product prices, and product names above your search results. What you're looking at is Google Shopping.

Google Shopping is a highly targeted source of buyer traffic if you use it right. That's because it's for people searching for **specific** products. They see the ad, the price, and a link that takes them right to that product. It's great traffic for bringing buyers to your drop ship site.

Traffic Source #2: Bing Shopping

The next one is Bing Shopping. Not as popular as Google, but another shopping engine where you can list products in a similar fashion.

Traffic Source #3: Facebook Ads

Facebook Ads for eCommerce can be pretty tricky. It's great for retargeting though. This means that if someone comes to your eCommerce store and they don't buy anything, you could show them an ad on Facebook with your store as a reminder.

You're basically telling them,"Hey, come back! We still have these items here for sale. We're still here. Come and purchase from us."

For new traffic, Facebook can work, but it's a much longer sales process. If someone finds you on Google Shopping, they were *searching* for the product that you're advertising.

If they find you on Facebook Ads, it's because you're trying to *target* them with an ad for your drop shipping store. The person on

Facebook isn't proactively searching and ready to buy. However, Facebook Ads can work if you build a **sales funnel** to turn them into buyers.

Traffic Source #4: Pinterest

The next thing you should do is use Pinterest. Pinterest is great for eCommerce because it gives your drop shipping site a ton of traffic and it's free.

Pinterest also has paid advertising. Even with just organic pins, Pinterest drives a lot of traffic to your drop shipping site. They even allow you to sell your drop ship products through Pinterest–linking directly to your Shopify store.

Traffic Source #5: Search Engine Optimization

Search engine optimization (SEO) is something I could speak about for hours and hours. However, with your drop shipping stores, SEO is not that hard since you aren't trying to rank for generic niche keywords. You're ranking for specific product titles. It's very easy to rank for something like a manufacturer name, product name, or SKU (stock keeping unit) number.

We're not going for those top level, super competitive keywords. We don't want that super competitive keyword traffic, because it's not buyer traffic.

If someone searches for chandeliers and they find our store, that's great, but they're probably not ready to buy. If they search for a specific chandelier company manufacturer name, product name or SKU, there's a good chance they're much further along in the buying cycle. That means we have a much better chance of turning that visitor into a customer.

Traffic Source #6: Guest Blog Posts

The next thing you could do is write guest blog posts. To do that, you need to find blogs that are relevant to your niche and share information on them. Most of the time, the owner of the blog will link back to your drop shipping site. This will help you get noticed by the blog's audience and search engines.

Traffic Source #7: Banner Ads

The next thing you should do to get buying traffic to you store, is take out banner ads on different blogs that are in your drop shipping niche.

Rent some advertising space, create a little graphic to be placed on the blog, and people will click it. It's a great way to get your drop shipping store noticed.

Traffic Source #8: Gift Card Giveaway

You could also do a gift card giveaway. If you're selling expensive items (like I recommend), your profit margin per sale should be relatively high. That means you can afford to give $25-$50 off per order.

A gift card giveaway is something that works really well, especially when launching a new drop ship store. Run a promotional contest for $50 gift cards that are valid on purchases of $1,000 or more. You still make a great amount of money and it's a great way to drive people to your store when you're first starting.

These are just a few traffic sources that I use. Now that we've covered some of the basics about getting traffic to your drop shipping store, let's talk about the most important part of the equation: **who will you market your product to?**

Identifying Your Market Segment

If you've been working through this book chronologically, you probably have a good idea of what it takes to make it in this business.

You know what drop shipping is. You know how much you can expect to make selling products. You know how to go about finding a niche to sell in, and you have an idea of how to start building your store...

But there's something missing. We know all about the importance of selecting a niche, but what about the *specifics*? Shouldn't we look at WHO we will be selling to?

Shouldn't we examine WHO our ideal customer is– their likes, dislikes, and preferences? Absolutely! That's where creating a customer avatar comes into play.

Try imagining starting a store, not knowing WHO your ideal customer is...

- You do your niche research...

- You get approved by legit suppliers...

- You successfully build an online store...

- Your website looks beautiful...

But...You find that your ads and marketing campaigns aren't converting like they should! Your email campaigns aren't converting well, and potential customers practically flee from your website upon entering.

The situations laid out above are classic cases of stores suffering from *"Zero WHO"* syndrome.

Zero WHO Syndrome

This happens when companies know their niche audience, but they don't *really* know who they're selling to. How does their ideal customer think? What does their ideal customer like to do? What are the customer's dreams? Let's say you're selling in the home improvement niche. Now, what information do you find more useful?

1. You are selling home improvement products to people who want to fix their homes or...

2. You are selling to males, age 31-50, who are looking to settle down and craft the perfect fixer upper. Your ideal customer probably reads *Family Handyman* is his spare time, and he enjoys working on his house or in the yard when he's not working the 9-5.

Which option seems more helpful to you as the store owner? Probably **option #2** right? The **first** piece of information just tells you a bit about your niche. This generic information is indeed necessary, but it's not very useful.

The **second** piece of information tells us a bit more. It reveals a bit about the demographic (gender, age) we are catering to. It shows us what type of media and information your customer adheres to (*Family Handyman* magazine), and it shows what our ideal customer does in his spare time (working in the yard and on his home).

Can you see how powerful this information could be? If you have information like this, you KNOW what your customer wants. You know what they are looking for in a product and how to reach them!

As a marketer (yes, you ARE a marketer), information is your greatest weapon. The more information you have, the more *value* you can provide to your customers.

The more value you can provide, the more *sales* you will make. Sounds nice, right?

What value does your product provide?

_____

_____

How will your product help people?

_____

_____

Who is your product for?

_____

_____

The Customer Avatar: What is it?

A customer avatar is a model of your ideal customer. It's a fictional buyer persona that we as drop shippers create in order to effectively target our customers.

Think of a crafting a customer avatar as doing target market research. A customer avatar is meant to cover as many relevant details as possible.

Why is Having a Customer Avatar Important?

The purpose of creating a customer avatar is to hone in your marketing tactics. The better we know our target market, the more sales we make.

How successful do you think you're going to be if you don't set a target? How will you properly adapt to the market if you don't *really* know who your target buyer is?

A customer avatar affects EVERY part of the sales and marketing process: email campaigns, content, web copy, ads, and much, much more.

Every part of the marketing process is influenced by your customer avatar, or lack thereof. Do you want to go in to drop shipping blind, not knowing WHO you're selling to or WHY you're selling to them?

Or do you wish to strategize and attack the market with confidence? The choice is yours...

Following is an example of a customer avatar in the home improvement niche:

Demographics		Hopes, Fears, & Barriers to Entry	
Customer Avatar Name: Handy Hank			
Age	32	**Hopes**	"I want to build something lasting."
Gender	Male		"I want tools that I can rely on."
Marital	Married		
# of Children	2		"I want equipment exactly when I need it."
Age of	2 and 3		
Location	Tyler, Texas	**Fears**	"I'll never be able to finish my projects."
Occupation	City Planner		"My equipment won't be worth the cost."
Motto	"Work is what you make it. Enjoy life, and work hard."		
Annual	$75,000		"There's so much work, but so little time."
Education	Bachelor's Degree		
Interests & Sources of Information		**Barriers to Entry**	"The cost of these tools is a bit too much to take on ..."
Magazines	Family Handyman, GQ, Esquire		"The skills needed for this project are highly advanced."
Books	*The Good Dad, Darth Vader and Son*		"I don't trust tool companies. They are all just trying to make a quick buck."
Blogs	Essential Home and Garden		

Gurus	Chip Gaines, Brett McKay	**Goals & Values**
Communicati	Email	

Objections & Role	**What are the future goals of Handy Hank?**
Handy Hank's role in the purchase process:	Support his family and take care of them.
Handy Hank discusses all purchases with his wife first. They are providing for two kids, so while money isn't tight, it definitely doesn't	Grow in other skills outside of work.
	Feel fulfilled with the work he accomplishes.
Handy Hank's objections to a particular purchase:	**What are Handy Hank's values in life?**
Product reviews online hold a lot of clout. If reviews are bad, Handy Hank won't buy the product.	Knows that family comes first.
If a website looks even a bit sketchy, Handy Hank will find a different store. He wants to trust those he does business with.	Is committed to quality and sustainability.

Notes:

_____

_____

_____

_____

_____

Building Your Customer Avatar in 5 Steps

Step 1: List the Hopes, Fears, and Barriers to Entry of Your Target Audience

Let's start off small. It's important to not rush creating your customer avatar. Pretend like you're *actually* getting to know someone. Be patient, and think things through.

Step 1 is all about getting the feel for your customer. Basically we are asking "What do you want, and how can I solve your problem?" We are looking into **their** mind for a moment so that **we** can give them something of value.

Hopes:

What does your customer want? What do they REALLY want? If a product could solve one of their most annoying problems, what product would that be?

Knowing the hopes of your customer helps you identify WHO your ideal customer really is. If your product won't solve an individual's problems, they will NOT be part of your customer avatar.

The services you provide are valuable to people! Find THOSE people. Target the person whose problems you will solve all day long.

Examples of Customer Hopes

- "I want to make my routine easier to accomplish."

- "I want to spend less time worrying about [their problem], and spend more time with my family."

- "I want to live my dream instead of dealing with [their problem]."

Fears:

What does your ideal customer fear the most? If you can tackle this fear, they will love you. Believe me. They will look to you as an ally– not as a retailer. They will keep coming back to you because you are an authority on solving *their* problems.

Examples of Customer Fears

- "I don't want to waste all of my time with [their problem]."

- "I'm afraid I'll never be able to [one of their hopes] because I'm always [their problem]."

- "If I'm not able to solve [their problem], I'll never be able to keep progressing and get better."

Barriers to Entry:

Even if you know nothing about business, you probably know what *barriers to entry* are. They are anything that get in the way of obtaining success (or hopes).

Examples of Customer Barriers to Entry

- "I have too much on my plate, and I have no time to research products I know will improve my life."

- "I'm spending so much money right now, and I'm having trouble keeping up with payments."

- "I don't know about [an industry]. They seem pushy to me, and I'm not looking to give them my hard earned money."

Creating Your Customer Avatar

In the back of this, find Your Customer Avatar and write out *five points each* for Hopes, Fears, and Barriers to entry. Try to write them from the customer's perspective. It helps. Reference back to this page when building your customer avatar.

Step 2: Assign Demographics and a Name

It's time to breathe some life into your avatar. Assigning a target demographic is extremely helpful. Knowing your customer's demographic helps you make effective decisions on ad platforms (Facebook, Twitter, etc.). When we add demographic info, our goal is to make the customer seem *real*.

Useful Demographic Information:

- Occupation
- Age
- Gender
- Children? Age of children?
- Location
- Motto (a principle your customer lives by in their words)
- Marital Status
- Job title
- Annual Income
- Education

Feel free to assign any other information, but the points above should provide a solid basis. We want to be as specific as possible when listing demographic info. Imagine that this customer truly exists. Are you starting to picture them? Do you know what they look like? If so, try coming up with a name.

Think of a name that fits the information you've compiled thus far. Maybe names like *Handy Hank* or *Ted Buyer* or *Veronica Market* will fit. Just pick a name that's memorable and fitting. Fill that out along with the demographics section of your customer avatar.

Step 3: Assign Goals and Values

What are the future goals of your ideal customer? How are they relevant to your products and services? Are they?

Examples of Goals

- He wants to save time on menial daily tasks.

- He wants to make money doing what he loves.

- He wants to build up an awesome portfolio.

What are this person's values in life? Let's look at what keeps our customer moving when all else fails. What does this person stand for?

Examples of Values

- She hopes to help those around her grow.

- She is committed to providing for her family.

- She never cuts corners on her projects.

As you can see, we're filling in the blanks of our customer avatar, and it's all starting to come together. Our avatar is beginning to feel real. Think of the potential of the information we've already compiled.

We know how to target our customer in email campaigns, we know what they want and what they want to run away from, and we know a few of the values that they will always abide by. Let's keep going. Our avatar isn't *quite* there yet.

Step 4: Comprise a List of Interests and How Your Customer Gets Their Information

We need to further personalize our customer avatar. Before we make an effort to communicate with our ideal customer, we should know how this person *absorbs* information. We need to know their likes, dislikes, and preferences when it comes to media and communication. I recommend listing:

- Top magazines in the niche

- Favorite books relating to niche or to customer's values

- What blogs your customer frequents

- What conferences they go to

- List of "gurus" or mentors that are relevant in their field

- How they prefer to communicate and receive information

If we can pin down Step 4, our customer avatar will provide us with valuable media insight. This step lets us see how to best approach our target customer when it comes to content and communication. This information helps us know what headlines, types of emails, and what kind of verbiage our customer positively responds to.

Remember, the more specific the better. Pick magazines, gurus, and blogs that are extremely niche specific. Pick unique media that pertains *specifically* to your customer's demographic.

Step 5: Address the Customer's Purchase Process

Visitors to your drop shipping site either purchase the product… or they don't. Your target customer will either move on, or they will spend money in your store. It's reality. You may think that this goes without saying, but these customer decisions are much deeper than many realize.

There are reasons why your target customer would buy and why they would walk away. Knowing these reasons will help you understand what you can do better to complete the sale.

Your Customer's Role in the Purchase Process

Address how your customer makes his or her decisions. What's their role in the purchase process? Is their decision the main factor when it comes to purchasing your product or service, or do they have to consult with a boss or spouse before spending that cash?

Knowing the *decision power* of your ideal customer lets you strategize your approach. This way, you meet them where THEY are at.

Objections to Purchase

On the other hand, **it's vital** to understand what's holding your customer back. Why wouldn't they buy your product? What are those last minute hesitations they have before clicking the "Confirm Purchase" button? These objections could sound something like:

- "Is this product necessary to my success?"

- "I don't know if this product meets my quality standards."

- "I'm not sure if this is an impulse buy, or if I REALLY need this…"

The sooner you can qualm and address these objections to purchase, the sooner you'll build a trusting relationship with your customer that results in more sales!

Finalize

You now have a completed customer avatar, which will be the beginning of your customer strategy. Use this as a roadmap when communicating to your customer.

Yes, you *will* sell to those who aren't the embodiment of your customer avatar. Creating an avatar gives you a solid target market. It is a way to keep your vision consistent and your message clear.

Lead Value Optimization

What's really important is converting your traffic into sales. Taking a visitor, having them go through your checkout page, and order from you. Traffic without sales doesn't mean anything. I don't care if you have a thousand people visit your site every hour. If you're not making sales, it doesn't matter.

Lead value optimization (LVO) is getting the most value out of the visitors that come to your site. Instead of just trying to increase buyer traffic, we are trying to get our leads to **buy more of our product.**

1. Let people know that your store sells more stuff or that you have products for sale elsewhere! Whether they abandoned their cart, or if they bought from you once before, it's always good to cross promote your stores and send a reminder.

2. You can earn extra money by doing some affiliate marketing, and you can gain customers from a related audience when you cross promote affiliate stores.

3. nformation products offer real value to potential customers.

4. Offering purchase add-ons is a great way to make more money, enhance value, and gain returning visitors.

5. Intangible upsell add-ons... what is this? Warranties, expedited shipping... these are add-ons that can definitely enhance the customer experience. The customer is happy, and you're a few bucks richer.

Most visitors to your site will not be ready to buy anything. This is where LVO comes in. The small percentage of people who are willing to buy products are the ones we truly focus on.

We make sure that they don't forget to check out. We make sure that they aren't missing out on anything that could be of value to them.

With LVO, we are attempting to provide a true service to our customer. We target them with remarketing tactics, upsells, implement tracking pixels, and more.

This isn't to spam them. These techniques aren't done to intentionally bother people. If you do LVO properly, your customer will come back. Why? You're offering them a quality service that will help them in some way.

Congratulations!

If you haven't already, it is time to put your newfound knowledge into action! You can do this.

You deserve a second stream of income that is completely controlled by you, one that you can work on whenever you choose and take a break from whenever you choose.

Or, if your goal is to create an online stream of income that can replace your 9 to 5 entirely so you can quit your job, you can achieve that as well – and you'll get it if you work hard and follow my system.

When I was first starting out in the drop shipping industry, I remember how overwhelming the process of building an online business was.

One of the key things that enabled me to achieve success was ignoring the "I need to build a business" thought, and just focusing on the very next step I knew I had to take…the little, but important next action that would take me that much closer to realizing my goal.

So, whether you're feeling overwhelmed by this or whether you're just excited and ready to get started, take that very next step.

And then the next one after that. And before you know it, you'll be looking back at how far you've come as a successful business owner and entrepreneur.

RESOURCES

Niche Selection Checklist

I can't stress it enough; choosing your product's niche is brutally important when building your drop shipping store. If building your website is like building the first floor on a building, choosing your niche is like laying the foundation.

When you are choosing a niche, you're choosing products that exist within a **specific market.** These products are exclusive and specific to a *small portion* of the entire online market (e.g., a site that sells straight razors **vs** Amazon).

My proven framework for drop shipping calls for a certain criteria when we are selecting niches:

• **Price** If you want to make money, we need to sell expensive products. Aim for niches with products priced at $200 and above.

• **Market** Look for products to sell online to upper-middle class single people or families with disposable income. These people are used to shopping online and comfortable making large purchases over the internet.

• **Brand** Avoid selling products that customers already have brand loyalty for. It's hard to convince people who are looking for a specific brand to shop generic instead.

• **Shipping** Shipping can be expensive but a winning combo is a high-priced product that has low shipping weights.

Use this section to brainstorm any niches that you think might be good for drop shipping. Make a list of at *least* 50 and record how they meet the niche criteria above.

Niche Idea: _____

Price:_____ Market: _____ Brand: _____ Shipping: _____

Notes: _____

_____

Niche Idea: _____

Price:_____ Market: _____ Brand: _____ Shipping: _____

Notes: _____

_____

Niche Idea: _____

Price:_____ Market: _____ Brand: _____ Shipping: _____

Notes: _____

_____

Niche Idea: _____

Price:_____ Market: _____ Brand: _____ Shipping: _____

Notes: _____

_____

Niche Idea: _____

Price:_____ Market: _____ Brand: _____ Shipping: _____

Notes: _____

_____

Niche Idea: _____

Price:_____ Market: _____ Brand: _____ Shipping: _____

Notes: _____

_____

Niche Idea: _____

Price:_____ Market: _____ Brand: _____ Shipping: _____

Notes: _____

_____

Niche Idea: _____

Price:_____ Market: _____ Brand: _____ Shipping: _____

Notes: _____

_____

Niche Idea: _____

Price:_____ Market: _____ Brand: _____ Shipping: _____

Notes: _____

_____

Niche Idea: _____

Price:_____ Market: _____ Brand: _____ Shipping: _____

Notes: _____

_____

Niche Idea: _____

Price:_____ Market: _____ Brand: _____ Shipping: _____

Notes: _____

_____

Niche Idea: _____

Price:_____ Market: _____ Brand: _____ Shipping: _____

Notes: _____

_____

Niche Idea: _____

Price:_____ Market: _____ Brand: _____ Shipping: _____

Notes: _____

_____

Niche Idea: _____

Price:_____ Market: _____ Brand: _____ Shipping: _____

Notes: _____

_____

Niche Idea: _____

Price:_____ Market: _____ Brand: _____ Shipping: _____

Notes: _____

_____

Niche Idea: _____

Price:_____ Market: _____ Brand: _____ Shipping: _____

Notes: _____

_____

Niche Idea: _____

Price:_____ Market: _____ Brand: _____ Shipping: _____

Notes: _____

_____

Niche Idea: _____

Price:_____ Market: _____ Brand: _____ Shipping: _____

Notes: _____

_____

Niche Idea: _____

Price:_____ Market: _____ Brand: _____ Shipping: _____

Notes: _____

_____

Niche Idea: _____

Price:_____ Market: _____ Brand: _____ Shipping: _____

Notes: _____

_____

Niche Idea: _____

Price:_____ Market: _____ Brand: _____ Shipping: _____

Notes: _____

_____

Niche Idea: _____

Price:_____ Market: _____ Brand: _____ Shipping: _____

Notes: _____

_____

Niche Idea: _____

Price:_____ Market: _____ Brand: _____ Shipping: _____

Notes: _____

_____

Niche Idea: _____

Price:_____ Market: _____ Brand: _____ Shipping: _____

Notes: _____

_____

Niche Idea: _____

Price:_____ Market: _____ Brand: _____ Shipping: _____

Notes: _____

_____

Niche Idea: _____

Price:_____ Market: _____ Brand: _____ Shipping: _____

Notes: _____

_____

Niche Idea: _____

Price:_____ Market: _____ Brand: _____ Shipping: _____

Notes: _____

_____

Niche Idea: _____

Price:_____ Market: _____ Brand: _____ Shipping: _____

Notes: _____

_____

Niche Idea: _____

Price:_____ Market: _____ Brand: _____ Shipping: _____

Notes: _____

_____

Niche Idea: _____

Price:_____ Market: _____ Brand: _____ Shipping: _____

Notes: _____

_____

Niche Idea: _____

Price:_____ Market: _____ Brand: _____ Shipping: _____

Notes: _____

_____

Niche Idea: _____

Price:_____ Market: _____ Brand: _____ Shipping: _____

Notes: _____

_____

Niche Idea: _____

Price:_____ Market: _____ Brand: _____ Shipping: _____

Notes: _____

_____

Niche Idea: _____

Price:_____ Market: _____ Brand: _____ Shipping: _____

Notes: _____

_____

Niche Idea: _____

Price:_____ Market: _____ Brand: _____ Shipping: _____

Notes: _____

_____

Niche Idea: _____

Price:_____ Market: _____ Brand: _____ Shipping: _____

Notes: _____

_____

Niche Idea: _____

Price:_____ Market: _____ Brand: _____ Shipping: _____

Notes: _____

_____

Niche Idea: _____

Price:_____ Market: _____ Brand: _____ Shipping: _____

Notes: _____

_____

Niche Idea: _____

Price:_____ Market: _____ Brand: _____ Shipping: _____

Notes: _____

_____

Niche Idea: _____

Price:_____ Market: _____ Brand: _____ Shipping: _____

Notes: _____

_____

Niche Idea: _____

Price:_____ Market: _____ Brand: _____ Shipping: _____

Notes: _____

_____

Niche Idea: _____

Price:_____ Market: _____ Brand: _____ Shipping: _____

Notes: _____

_____

Niche Idea: _____

Price:_____ Market: _____ Brand: _____ Shipping: _____

Notes: _____

_____

Niche Idea: _____

Price:_____ Market: _____ Brand: _____ Shipping: _____

Notes: _____

_____

Niche Idea: _____

Price:_____ Market: _____ Brand: _____ Shipping: _____

Notes: _____

_____

Niche Idea: _____

Price:_____ Market: _____ Brand: _____ Shipping: _____

Notes: _____

_____

Niche Idea: _____

Price:_____ Market: _____ Brand: _____ Shipping: _____

Notes: _____

_____

Niche Idea: _____

Price:_____ Market: _____ Brand: _____ Shipping: _____

Notes: _____

_____

Niche Idea: _____

Price:_____ Market: _____ Brand: _____ Shipping: _____

Notes: _____

_____

Niche Idea: _____

Price:_____ Market: _____ Brand: _____ Shipping: _____

Notes: _____

_____

Niche Idea: _____

Price:_____ Market: _____ Brand: _____ Shipping: _____

Notes: _____

_____

Niche Idea: _____

Price:_____ Market: _____ Brand: _____ Shipping: _____

Notes: _____

_____

Niche Idea: _____

Price:_____ Market: _____ Brand: _____ Shipping: _____

Notes: _____

_____

Niche Idea: _____

Price:_____ Market: _____ Brand: _____ Shipping: _____

Notes: _____

_____

Niche Idea: _____

Price:_____ Market: _____ Brand: _____ Shipping: _____

Notes: _____

_____

Competitor Research Table

After you identified several niches that match the criteria, you'll want to check out the competition. You should base this decision on where they are ranking on Google (higher is better), how many brands they carry (the more brands, the better), and how user friendly and appealing their site design is.

You want to make sure you find at least three competitor websites for each niche. If you can't find competitors, then it's probably time to start over with a different niche.

Niche	Competitor Store Name	
Notes:		

Niche	Competitor Store Name	
Notes:		

Niche	Competitor Store Name	

Notes:

Niche	Competitor Store Name	

Notes:

Niche	Competitor Store Name	

Notes:

Niche	Competitor Store Name	

Notes:

Niche	Competitor Store Name	

Notes:

Niche	Competitor Store Name	

Notes:

Niche	Competitor Store Name	
Notes:		

Niche	Competitor Store Name	
Notes:		

Niche	Competitor Store Name	
Notes:		

Niche	Competitor Store Name	

Notes:

Niche	Competitor Store Name	

Notes:

Niche	Competitor Store Name	

Notes:

Competitor Analysis

Once you discover who your competitors are, you will need to analyze the top three stores, in terms of function and design, and decide what you could use from them, or what you shouldn't use from them.

You will also need to see what social media platforms your competitors are using. For example, your competition has an Instagram account with the last post being six months ago, this might be a sign that they do not get conversions from Instagram.

You need to know your competition anyway, but this practice will also help you build a well designed and optimized selling machine!

Find the Top Three Competitors in Your Niche:

_____

_____

_____

List Three Things They Do Well:

_____

_____

_____

List Three Things They Do Poorly:

_____

_____

What Social Media Platforms are Your Competitors Actively Using?

Other Things to Consider:

What does their logo look like? Is it simple or intricate?

What is their store and domain name?

What does their "About Me" page say?

Where do they list their phone number? Are they easy to contact?

_____

_____

_____

How do they interact with their customers? Do they offer customer ratings on products?

_____

_____

_____

_____

_____

Notes:

_____

_____

_____

_____

_____

_____

_____

Your Customer Avatar

Demographics	
Customer Avatar Name:	
Age	
Gender	
Marital Status	
# of Children	
Age of Children	
Location	
Occupation	
Motto	
Annual Income	
Education	

Interests & Sources of Information	
Magazines	
Books	
Blogs	
Gurus	
Communication	

Objections & Role in Purchase Process

Your customer's role in the purchase process:

Your customer's objections to a particular purchase:

Hopes, Fears, & Barriers to Entry

Hopes	
Fears	
Barriers to Entry	

Goals & Values

What are the future goals of your ideal customer?

What are your customer's values in life?

Glossary

Affiliate: A person who promotes a seller's products on their website or blog(s)– in return, any purchase made through the affiliate link will result in a commission to the affiliate.

Affiliate Links: A URL link that an affiliate uses to sell a company's products or services. That link can be tracked by the company whose products are being sold; this way, the company knows which sales came from the affiliate.

Alibaba: China's biggest and most notorious eCommerce company.

Amazon: One of the world's largest online retailers. Amazon is also a cloud service provider.

Authorization: A transaction to determine the ownership of a service, platform, account or any other item on which one user has rights over.

Arbitrage: Buying commodities at a low price, and then reselling them at a high price.

Back-end: Pertains to servers and databases– the infrastructure that makes the site work.

Blog: An online publication that is used to either disperse information or market products and services.

Bounce Rate: A stat that displays the percentage of users on your website who navigated away from the site after only looking at a single page.

Brick and Mortar Store: A retailer who has a physical location. Drop shippers should not try to compete with brick and mortar stores.

Call-to-Action (CTA): A marketing technique that asks an audience or reader to take action by interacting with something. This action– could be clicking a URL, writing a note, voicing a thought– is meant to lead to a desired result.

Chargeback: When a customer issues a chargeback, their bank forcibly takes the funds from you (the merchant), issuing it back to the customer. In order to do this, the customer must make a claim that they were unable to return the product, that the product was deficient, or that the you did not fulfill their order

Content Management System (CMS): Software that manages the editing and creation process of a website. This is where you manage your store.

Conversion: A stat showing the percentage of people reached that enter into a tier of your marketing campaign. For instance, if you had 10,000 people on an email list and you convert 100 to purchase a product, the conversion rate would be 1%

Cookie: Sites use cookies to keep track of a user's habits. They are small files that are saved onto your computer.

Digital Nomad: Someone who can accomplish their work anywhere with an internet connection. Digital nomads are location-independent and usually travel from place to place.

Directories: Websites that link to other retailers, stores, or sites.

Distributor: A middleman. They buy products from the supplier and then sell the products to drop shippers.

Domain: The URL of a website (i.e. for https://www.dropshiplifestyle.com/, the domain name is dropshiplifestyle.com)

Domain Name System (DNS): Translates your domain name into an IP address. Basically, it fetches your website from a server.

Drop Shipping: A retail method where you don't keep products in stock. Instead, you partner with a supplier that stocks its own inventory. You transfer customer orders and shipment details to them, and the supplier ships the order directly to the customer.

eBay: An extremely popular online selling platform and marketplace, best known for its consumer-to-consumer sales.

eCommerce: Short for "electronic commerce," eCommerce is the act of selling or buying things on the internet.

Expedited Shipping: Form of shipping that arrives to the customer faster than a standard shipped item. Usually products that are expedited require a fee that is more expensive than standard shipping.

Front-end: The client-side and "web design" aspect of a site. It's what the user sees.

Fulfillment: After your customer makes an order, you need to ship it. This process is referred to in Shopify as order fulfillment.

Google Trends: A tool that displays search analytics for particular terms or keywords searched on Google.

HTML (Hyper Text Markup Language): Standard markup language for creating web pages and applications.

Internet Retailer: This is you, the drop shipper. In drop shipping, the internet retailer sells the product, and the supplier provides and ships the product.

Javascript: Scripting language that is used on web pages.

Landing Pages: Sales page on a website meant to increase conversion rates.

Liquidation: When a store intentionally gets rid of products– usually by offering sales.

Logistics: The behind the scenes magic of the inventory and shipping processes.

Long-Tail (Marketing): Refers to niche markets that doesn't primarily exist in the mainstream markets or media.

Long-Tail (Traffic): Web traffic that comes from SEO targeted keywords that are long and specific.

MAP Pricing: Minimum advertised price. This is the lowest price a supplier will let you sell their products for.

Margins: What you make after all is said and done. Your net revenue from a sale (i.e., what you make after shipping and wholesale costs).

Middlemen: Another party between your store and the supplier who you buy products from. You want to avoid middlemen. Working directly with the supplier is the best way to uphold quality and customer service.

Net Profit: Revenue minus business expenses.

Niche: A small, targeted market where specific items are sold.

Organic Views: When people find your site directly by searching for it themselves. They don't go through an ad, Facebook, or an affiliate link.

Outsourcing: Hiring out tasks to individuals or companies outside of your business.

Overhead Cost: Cost of running your business.

Pay Per Click (PPC): Every time a user clicks one of your ads, this is the rate you'll pay.

Restocking Fee: A fee that some suppliers charge the customer if products are returned.

Search Engine Optimization (SEO): Optimizing your online content ranks to impact how it ranks on search engines. One can optimize their website by using certain phrases and keywords.

Search Engine Results Page (SERP): This is an analysis of what the first page of a search engine looks like for a given keyword.

Social Media Marketing: Marketing products or services with social media.

Sole Proprietorship: A form of business where there is little legal difference between the owner and the actual business.

Split Testing: A marketing technique where different variables are tested on an audience to gauge results that will *hopefully* be repeatable.

Supply Chain: Think of this as the hands that a product must travel through to get to a customer.

Tracking Number: A code that is usually included with a product. It reveals where the product is and when it will arrive to the customer.

Trade Show: Manufacturers take products to physical locations (trade shows) for retailers like you to see.

Turnkey Stores: These are 'ready to go' drop shipping stores sold on low-end auction websites. It's a quick way for sellers to make a buck. Usually a huge waste of time and money for the buyer.

Wholesale Price: The price that the supplier offers YOU, the retailer on products. You buy the products at wholesale, and then you sell them for more to make a profit.

Wholesaler: Another word for your supplier.

NOTES:

_____

_____

_____

_____

_____

_____

_____

_____

_____

_____

_____

_____

52361173R00085

Made in the USA
Middletown, DE
10 July 2019